OUR FIRST

Lady Pope

Victor Villaseñor

Waterside Press
2055 Oxford Ave
Cardiff, CA 92007
http://www.waterside.com

Dedicated to
Our First Lady Pope
and to
Grandmothers Worldwide
Women of Substance

Women of Power
Who are the Key for Uniting All of Humanityand helping Us Heal our
Beloved Mother Earth, and thusly take us
off the Most Endangered Species List.

Dear Reader

Thank you for picking up this book. This is no accident. In fact, we're right on schedule, because deep within our Collective Cellular Soul there is GIGANTIC GLOBAL HOPE for us to now reclaim our Feminine Energy and create a kinder more loving world of daily miracles!

Please email me victor@victorvillasenor.com. to continue the dialogue.

Thank you! *Gracias!*
Victor Villaseñor

QUOTES

"I know God will not give me anything I can't handle. I just wish that He didn't have so much trust in me."

Mother Teresa of Calcutta

"Before civilization you, me, we, all of us were like weeds, because a civilized plant like a rose you've got to feed and water and spray for bugs or it will die. But a wild uncivilized plant like a weed, you give it nothing and it lives. You poison it and it comes back the following year with the rains. You pour cement over it and it will break that concrete reaching for the sunlight of God. And this is how we, humans, all used to be all over the earth. Uncivilized and Wild of Heart, Alive of Soul, and Indestructible in Faith as we reached for the Sunlight of God!"

Doña Margarita

DEFINITIONS

From the Webster's New World Dictionary pre1990:

Genius: guardian deity, or spirit of a person; spirit, natural ability. According to ancient Roman belief, a guardian spirit is assigned to a person at birth.

Catholic: universal, all-inclusive; of general interest or value; hence, having broad sympathies or understanding; liberal.

Balance: an instrument for weighing, especially one that opposes equal weights, as in two matched scales hanging from either end of a lever supported exactly in the middle. The imaginary scales of fortune or fate, as an emblem of justice or the power to decide; hence, the power to decide human fate, value, etc. A state of bodily equilibrium: as he kept his balance on the tightrope. Equilibrium in design, painting, music composition, harmonious proportions. The constellation Libra, or the seventh sign of the zodiac.

God: Any of various beings as conceived as supernatural, immortal, and having special powers over the lives and affairs of people, and of course nature. An image that is worshipped. In monotheistic religions, the creator and ruler of the universal, regarded as eternal, infinite, all-powerful, and all-knowing; Supreme Being; Almighty.

Miracle: an event or action that apparently contradicts known scientific laws, and is hence thought to be due to supernatural causes, especially to an act of God. A remarkable event or thing. A marvel.

Angel: a messenger from God. A supernatural being, either good or bad, to whom is attributed more than human power, intelligence. A guiding spirit or influence.

From My Personally Created Dictionary

Godelution: the understanding that there is no contradiction between God and evolution or between God and science; they do, in fact, work together.

Follow Infront: the understanding that the big male snow geese who fly in front of the V-Formations of geese migrating north and south don't lead, but 'follow infront'. It's the female and young geese who set the pace and lead from behind.

VoyageDream: A dream in which you voyage and it really did occur.

INTRODUCTION
MIRACLE MAKERS

My little sister went racing out of the house, screaming, "Papa and Mama are here! Papa and Mama and Tencha are home!"

Tencha was our older sister and she and our parents had left for Mexico right after our older brother Joseph's funeral. I came running from the corrals when I heard my dad honking his car horn. I'd been feeding livestock and helping milk our cows and giving the warm sweet-smelling sticky milk to our calves out of a bucket.

That evening our mother took my little sister Linda and me aside and told us that she'd bought something from Mexico that was full of magic. My sister and I were all eyes as my mother took a little flat box out of her purse and began to unwrap it.

"This is a mango seed," she said to us full of enthusiasm.

The seed was oval shape and white dry and flat and about the size of my hand. I'd just turned nine and my sister Linda was five and we looked at each other. I guess we'd expected something like Indian jewelry or a stuffed frog with great big eyes.

"This seed comes from the sweetest, most beautiful mango I ever ate!" said our mother with a big smile.

"And it has magic?" asked my sister.

"Yes, you'll see," said our mother.

"Is it from deep in Mexico?" I asked.

"Yes, from right outside of Mazatlan, Sinaloa in a beautiful rich valley where I'm sure my mother's people once lived. You see," she said, handing us the big long seed, "I am going to nurture it and plant it with love and it's going to give us the most beautiful sweet mangos you have ever tasted!"

The seed had long little thin lines running its length and a rough feeling texture and tiny white whiskers along its edge. My sister and I took turns inspecting it and then handed it back to our mother. We were really disappointed.

But then I'll never forget, the next day when I came home from school my mother was in the kitchen pushing a little nail into the middle of the mango seed, and in each hole she'd made with the nail, she inserted a wooden toothpick, and all this time she was smiling and humming and singing and being so happy which was really good, because ever since my brother died our mother had mostly been crying.

Then after she'd inserted toothpicks all the way around the middle of the mango seed, she filled a small glass with water and put the mango seed length ways into the glass and the toothpicks only allowed the seed to submerge halfway into the water, because the long toothpicks stuck out beyond the rim of the glass. Then I'll never forget, my mother dropped a Bayer aspirin into the glass and I watched it go to the bottom and start to dissolve with little white smoke like lines going upward.

"There," said my mother, "the poor little seed got a headache with me poking holes in it, but now with its crown of toothpicks and my love, it will heal and flourish!"

Saying this, *mi mama* began making dinner and I changed clothes and hurried out to the corrals to help my dad and our workers feed livestock and milk cows.

Well, what can I say, for the rest of that school year I'd come home all excited to see my mother being so happy with her mango seed that she kept it on the windowsill above the kitchen sink. The seed began to grow long white whiskers that in no time filled the little jar. My mother explained to us that these were roots, and then one day she told me to get her some old dried out horse manure.

"Not cow manure," she said, "because it's too strong and these young roots are still too tender."

So that day I watched my mother plant her mango seed in a little pot with top soil and horse manure and talk and sing to it, explaining to the mango seed that yes, she was far from home, but with love and nourishment this could be her new home.

Then with summer coming and school ending, I was out with the horses with my dad and little sister almost all the time, so I all but forgot about the mango seed until one night after dinner our mother said, "I have a very important announcement to make and so I want you all to pay close attention."

There was just my dad and mother and sister Linda and me at the dinner table. Our older sister Tencha was living in San Diego.

"I want all of you to know that I've been taking my little mango plant and putting it in sunlight for a couple of hours every day, and now it's time for me to plant our little tree, so I'm going to start walking around our ranch and asking my little mango where it would like to live."

My little sister and I almost laughed, thinking it was really funny for our mother to be asking a plant where it wanted to live. But our dad coughed that special cough of his and we knew better than to laugh.

Our mother closed her eyes in concentration. "And I will not permit anyone to laugh or make fun of me and my little mango tree, because just as my mother taught me that all of God's Creation is Alive, you too will get to see this mango far from home grow big and flourish, because of all the love that I have shown it. So I say, not one snicker or joke, because this is a Sacred Holy Quest that I am on, just as my dear mother was able to do in the Rain of Gold canyon where so many others couldn't get their corn and string beans and squash to grow. Do you understand? Then once I plant this little tree, every day at three in the afternoon I will sing and give love to our little mango tree."

For over a week we saw our mother walking around our ranch talking to her little potted mango tree, asking the 8 inch tall plant if it felt at home at this place, or if it felt more at home at this other place.

Then one day after dinner, she informed us that she now knew where the little mango wanted to live.

"How do you know?" asked Linda.

"Because every time we get near this spot, her leaves pick up and begin to smile. Plants know where they want to nest just like birds," she added. "The place she chose is near the swimming pool area next to the driveway so she can get plenty of sunlight, and yet be close enough to the house so she wouldn't get lonely."

"Trees can get lonely?" asked Linda.

"Of course," said our mother, "all of Creation needs attentive love. My mother always told me that this is what we were sent to do here on Mother Earth, to help *Papito Dios* spread His Love*Amor* throughout all the rest of His Creation."

So we all helped our mother plant her little tree and she now began to water her tiny mango tree with a mixture of cow manure and other ingredients, and oh, wow, did that little tree take off like nobody's business, and within three years it was taller than me with strong little branches and a profusion of large dark leaves, then it began producing mangos. Big ones! Little ones! And all so colorful – red and yellow and orange, and a FRAGRANCE OF HEAVEN that you could smell all the way to my mother's rose garden in front of our home. And yes, they were the sweetest tasting mangos we'd ever tasted.

The years passed and it seemed like every other year our mango tree gave us – not just a few mangos - but a bumper crop of 100s of pounds of mangos, and yet different than in Mexico where mangos got ripe in the summer, our mangos didn't ripen until mid-October through late-November, because being this far north, I guess, they needed those extra days of sunlight in order to get ripe.

I married. We had two sons and one year we went to the huge San Diego County Fair in Del Mar to look at the livestock, see the horse shows, and ride the Ferris wheel. Then we were walking around seeing the sights when we came to a place that was selling young mango trees that they guaranteed would produce fruit, even this far north.

We stopped. My wife Barbara and our two sons David and Joseph all knew the story of my mother's miraculous mango tree.

"Do these really produce fruit?" I asked, fully realizing that most mango trees throughout Southern California didn't produce fruit and were used for ornament trees because of their big dark green leaves.

"Yes," said the man who was probably in his mid-fifties and was sitting alongside a younger man and woman. "Would you like to take one home?" he asked.

"Oh, no, thank you," I said. "We already have a mango tree at home that produces 100s of pounds of mangos, so many, in fact, that we can't eat them all."

"Impossible!" said the man, glancing at the woman and man beside him. He got to his feet. "Do you have any idea how long it takes for a tree or plant to acclimate to its environment before it can produce?"

"No, I don't," I said.

"Well, some scientists say that it took corn 100 years to move just a few miles north or south, so it literally took corn 100s of 1000s of years to acclimatize from its origin in Central America up into Mexico and North America and down to Peru and South America."

I could see that the man was upset.

"But my mother-in-law's mango tree does produce fruit," said Barbara.

I took Barbara's hand and glanced at our boys. My heart was pounding.

"Look," I said to the man, "we might not know anything about corn taking 100s of 1000s of years to acclimate, but we do know that the grandmother of these two boys has a mango tree that produces fruit every year, and a huge amount every other year." I took in a deep breath. "I was just a little boy back in 1949 when my parents went to Mexico and my mother came back with what she said was the seed of the sweetest mango she'd ever tasted, and she told us that she was going to do great magic with that mango seed just as she'd seen her own mother do miracles with corn and string beans up in the mountains of *Chihuahua*."

The man looked at me. Really looked at me and Barbara and our two sons.

"What's your mother's name?" he asked.

"Lupe," I said. "Lupe Villaseñor."

"Lupe Villaseñor!" he shouted. "That's what this strain of mango trees was originally called! All the mango producing fruit trees in South California, Arizona, and parts of New Mexico and Texas came from your mother's tree, but lately a grower's association is trying to take credit, because they say that without genetic altering no one could have developed a mango fruit bearing tree this far north. Does your mother live? Do you know how she did it?"

The man was nothing but smiles now.

"Yes, she lives," I said, "and yes, I know how she did it."

"Tell us," he said, turning to the man and woman beside him, "because you see, Charlie, the old man, who introduced us to this miracle tree, protected your mother's privacy so much that we didn't know if she even lived anymore."

"Charlie?" I said. "He was really old, right?"

"Yes, and he's passed."

"Well, I think I remember him coming to our house to see my mother now and then to get mango seeds and trimmings and they'd visit for hours."

"Oh, this is wonderful!" said the woman. "You see, we have basically devoted our lives to the natural procreation of exotic plants and your mother's mango is one of our cornerstones in our opposition to genetic alternation, which destroys the essence and food value of everything they touch."

And so I told them the whole story and how my mother had poured all her love into that mango seed with song and joy and then I explained how my mother had told me that her Yaqui Indian mother had done the same thing with her vegetable garden up on the mountain of Chihuahua.

"In fact, my mother explained to us," I said, "that women, that mothers, that grandmothers have been doing this for 100s of 1000s of years, if not millions, making a home for themselves, their family, and their plants wherever they went. And a home is where the Heart and Soul of our plants and family flourish!"

The two men and one woman were astonished.

"Well, this then sheds a whole new light on civilization," said the woman "And shows that maybe everything we knew about botany could be incorrect," said the young man, "and it didn't take a 100 years for corn to move a mile. Do you know from where in Mexico your mother brought her seed?"

"Yes, from a rich beautiful valley not far from Mazatlan, Sinaloa where she believed her mother's people had lived before they'd been, well, annihilated."

"We're her people Native Americans?"

"Yes," I said. "Yaqui."

"You know, we're just beginning to understand how Native people all over the world were excellent farmers with a sustainable relationship with nature. So, then, you are saying that your mother Lupe acclimated a mango well-over a 1000 miles from its origin in just a few years?"

"Yes," I said, "that's what happened."

"This is nothing short of a miracle," said the woman, "because then when tribes were migrating all over our planet, women were able to have their plants acclimate to their new environment within a couple of years. Do you see what this means? Women have been doing miracles for 100s of 1000s of years!"

"Yes, that's how I was raised," I said, "with the understanding that women, who carry the seed of life, are our miracle makers and our natural leaders, and that men, like snow geese, who fly across the sky in V-Formations in their migration, 'follow infront' breaking the wind so that it then takes 30% less energy for the rest of the flock to keep up, and in this way we, Human People, are then in Tune with our Symphony of Creation that is Alive within the Holy Breath of God!"

"This is almost exactly what I was told by that group of Navajo women last year," said the woman.

So we visited a little longer, traded names, phone numbers, and then Barbara and I invited them to our home in South Oceanside, and left. All the way home our two boys were talking about nothing else but miracles and they were so happy and all excited. And I could now see that my mother had been absolutely right when she'd told my little sister Linda and me she'd brought us something from Mexico that was full of magic.

And this is exactly what this book *Our First Lady Pope* is really all about, that the time has come in our "Godelution" for all of us, Collectively, to unite together and then BINGO! We can begin to see the larger picture and Women of Substance, Women of Power can unite the whole world over, and once more Consciously become Miracle Makers!

You see, according to the Mayan Calendar, our Mother Earth has been working in Harmony with the Universe in increments of 26,000 years for millions of years and we are just finishing up our last 26,000 years of Aggressive Global Masculine Energy and are now moving into 26,000 years of Compassionate Global Feminine Energy. In other words, there's nothing we can do to stop World Harmony and Peace and Abundance for All! And this isn't a far-fetched dream, but the larger picture of reality with which I was raised by my Yaqui Indian grandmother.

So, dear reader, now please fasten your seatbelt and lets you, me, all of us take a "VoyageDream" of Cellular Memory past the Mother Moon and to the Furthest Stars within our very own "Kingdom of God" Back To The Future when we were All, All, All Indigenous People the world over, and we Knew Our Original Instructions!

Truly, understand that for all of us back then the question had never been 'Is there intelligent life on other planet?' The real question had always been 'When is there going to be intelligent life on this planet?' Ready? So let's go back to "yesteryear" when we, Human People, all lived within the larger picture, and so we were all full of wonder and magic, and happiness! BIG BIG HAPPINESS!

Thank you, *gracias*,
Victor E. Villaseñor

P.S. I'd like you to know that I started writing *Our First Lady Pope* in the late 1990s and early part of the 2000s, and it's the second volume of the trilogy of *Snow Goose Global Thanksgiving*, and the third volume is *She, Too, Walks On Water*, which I am currently finishing.

Also I'd like you to know that this second volume is an accumulation of not just what happened when I was invited to speak to a group of retired nuns and priests in upper state Wisconsin, but when I later spoke to sixteen different denominations of Christian ministers in Iowa and to a convent of nuns in Kentucky.

You see, my talk in Wisconsin burst open a dam within me and I was then able to accept invitations to speak at many Catholic high schools, universities, and religious conventions, including the global one in Seoul, South Korea of 2014, which I wasn't able to attend, because I'd previously accepted an invitation from the University of Benito Juarez in Oaxaca, México, my grandmother *Doña Margarita's* home region.

Also, if you'd like, look up Villaseñor Mango on your smart phone. You'll be surprised. *Hasta Luego!*

BOOK ONE

ONE

I was shocked.

A group of retired nuns and priests were inviting me to go and speak to them up by the Great Lakes near the Canadian border, but I didn't want to go. I mean, I hadn't written that well about the Catholic Church in my book *Rain of Gold*, and yet it was this very book that had caused these old nuns and priests to write to me. I decided to sleep on the matter as my dad had always done whenever he'd had an important decision to make, and in the morning, much to my surprise, I awoke with the realization that I still had a lot of love and even some good memories of the Church.

In fact, looking back I could now see that it had been the sounds and smells that had first caused me to fall in love with the Holy Roman Catholic Church. I'd just been a little kid, and the smell of the smoking incense, and the quiet sounds of the people praying, and the old deaf priest's large booming voice full of warm sing-song sounding- language, and then the altar boys singing back to the priest with beautiful high-sounding voices, pretending to also be speaking in Latin, but in actuality they'd be singing to the old priest in Spanish, telling him that they agreed with him and it was best to cook the wild turkey in Mexican green sauce. Oh, it had all been so much fun. The old priest dressed up in an elaborate dress like a queen and chanting with such seriousness, and the altar boys, also dressed in elaborate dresses, chanting back to him with so much *gusto*.

"Gua-jo-lote! Co-cido en sal-saaa verrr-de!" would chant the altar boys, and most parents would get mad, hearing that the boys were tricking the half-deaf old priest, but my dad would join us kids and sing along with the laughing, giggling altar boys.

Oh, it was the best show in town and these first wonderful memories began for me at Saint Patrick's Holy Catholic Church in the Mexican *barrio* of Carlsbad, California with the smell of burning incense being whirled about in a little silver bell, and the quiet rolling whispers of my mother and grandmother saying the rosary. Then, when I got a little older, it was the bells of Saint Mary's Star of the Sea in Oceanside, a few miles north from the *barrio* of Carlsbad, with which I fell in love. The loud-clanging bells, and the smell of the sea mixed with cutting flowers and incense, slightly different smells than the ones in Carlsbad, but the sounds of the people praying were exactly the same and wonderful.

Then came the San Luis Rey Mission, king of all the missions of California, with its great towering bell that could be heard across the whole valley full of luscious green fields and best of all the hundreds of beautiful goldfish in the water fountain right across from the entrance of the huge magnificent great-smelling mission where, on some lucky Sundays, we got to see wild pigeons flying about inside of the church as the old priest and the altar boys chanted back and forth to each other about the best way to cook wild turkey in Mexican green sauce.

And also, looking back, I could now see that it had felt very *especial* to get all dressed up every Sunday and listen to the sounds of the Holy Roman Catholic Church, and then get to go out for breakfast as one big happy hungry *familia* who'd confessed our sins, received Holy Communion, and were now all at peace with God Almighty, the Holy Creator of the whole Universe!

But still, for days, I procrastinated, because I just couldn't see myself going to see a bunch of retired nuns and priests. Hell, I could also still remember all the abuses that I'd received at Catholic school. What happened was that I'd been going to public school in South Oceanside just a few blocks from our home and everything had been going... well, not too bad, until I got to the third grade, then I just couldn't seem to be able to learn how to read.

I mean, reading in second grade had been difficult enough for me, but reading in third grade had just been beyond my comprehension. School became a nightmare. The kids began making fun of me. I became a bed wetter. And I flunked the third grade, but I was also told not to worry, that by taking the third grade over, I'd surely learn how to read. But I didn't, and this was when even my best friends began to call me stupid and explained to me that it was because I was a Mexican.

Then I flunked the third grade for a second time, and kids began to throw rocks at me and wait for me after school so they could beat me up. I got mad and would grab and bite and scratch the kids and my parents were called in and my teacher told them that I was always getting into fights. And this was when my parents told my teacher to pass me on to the fourth grade, and they'd then take me out of public school and put me in Catholic school out at the San Luis Rey Mission.

At first the teacher said she couldn't do that, but then when my dad leaned in so close to her with his big smoking cigar and a lug of avocados with an envelope full of money, my teacher's eyes got so big with fear that she quickly agreed to pass me on. Then driving home my mother explained that the nuns and priests weren't Protestants and so they'd be kinder and more patient with me and so I'd be sure to learn how to read.

And my mom and dad were almost right, because Sister Theresa, the little nun who was assigned to teach me how to read after school, was wonderful and kind and never got mad at me when I didn't get it. Within a week I was in love with her and so one afternoon I asked her if she would marry me when I grew up.

She smiled, I'll never forget, and took my hand and explained to me that she was already married to Jesus.

"He's dead, you know," I said.

"Yes, but I'm married to Our Lord Jesus in spirit," she said, still smiling.

"Oh, that's okay," I said, "we can then get married in body and have babies.

"But she was never able to give me her answer, because just then the big, old Mother Superior came crashing through the door, screaming at me that I was the devil and slapped me so hard that she knocked me out of my chair, and then she went after my little nun, slapping her and slapping her. And this was when Sister Theresa's habit was knocked off of her head, and I saw that her long, beautiful dark red hair was the same color as my horse's mane and tail. And she was so young and beautiful and yet she wouldn't fight back or defend herself, and the big, old mother superior just kept hitting her.

This incident I would never forget. I'd only been eight years old, but still I'd been so full of love that I'd leaped up off the floor and attacked the smelly old Mother Superior, getting under her long robe and biting her leg and gouging my nails into her soft flesh. She screamed bloody murder and quit hitting my little nun and began hitting me on the head. But still I continued biting her until the priest came rushing in and grabbed me by my hair and dragged me down the hallway, then locked me in a broom closet. After that, I was never allowed to see my little nun again, and when months later I did see her, her face instantly filled with terror and she took off running.

My heart died. What had they done to her? And also after that incident, it was like the old mother superior and the priest now thought that they had an open license to beat me and after each beating explain to me that I'd been born with Original Sin, and so it was their sworn duty and for the good of my soul for them to beat me and keep me away from all the other kids.

And so no, no, no, now as an adult I couldn't see myself going to see any old, retired nuns and priests. After all, what I'd written about in *Rain of Gold* was that God was full of *amor*. Not wrath. And that every day was *otro milagro de Dios,* every day was another miracle given to us by God, and that our job here on Mother Earth was for us, five-pointed Walking Stars, to help Our Holy Creator plant His ongoing Sacred Garden of Heaven on Earth.

But then finally, after a few days of still not being able to make up my mind, I decided to just go across the grass, past the chicken coops, and see my mother who lived in our new, smaller house.

My dad had passed over ten years ago, and so I now spoke to my mother, who was almost 90 years old, but she'd never been much of a talker like my dad. To go to church and pray her rosary had always been more of my mother's style of how to deal with difficult situations. Getting to her house, her front door was open, which was okay. At our little *rancho* in South Oceanside we hardly ever locked our doors at night, and during the day we didn't close them half of the time.

"*Mama*," I called out as I went inside, "I'd like to speak with you."

"Okay," she called back, "I'm in the kitchen. I'm making myself a *quesadilla*. Would you like one?"

I'd already had breakfast about two hours ago, but still the thought of having one of my mother's delicious *quesadillas*, meaning a handmade *tortilla* folded in half with cheese in the middle, sounded pretty good.

"Yeah, sure," I said, licking my lips. "Do you also have avocado? I can go and pick a couple if you'd like."

"No, I already picked a few this morning," she said. "You slice one while I do the *quesadillas* on the *comal*."

"Okay," I said, and so I washed my hands, dried them, then began feeling the avocados to see which one was the ripest.

Sitting down with my mother, we ate our *quesadillas* with fresh slices of avocado and homemade *salsa*, then I came right to the point.

"*Mama*," I said, "I've been invited to go to Wisconsin up by the Great Lakes to give a talk to a bunch of old retired nuns and priests, but I don't know if I can go."

"Oh, you don't think you have warm enough clothes?" she said. "Well, that's no problem, *mijito*. Just do as your father always said he learned to do up in Montana and wear many layers. You'll be okay, *mijito*. Don't worry."

"*Mama*, I got the clothes. That's not the *problema*," I said. "The *problema* is that I was well, you know, abused by the nuns and priests out at the San Luis Rey Mission so much that part of me just doesn't want to go."

"But didn't you bite a nun? Isn't that what started the whole problem?" "Oh, *Mama*," I said, "I've told you a thousand times that that's not how it happened."

"Well, the priest, he told your father and me that you bit a nun so hard that they'd had to take her to the hospital."

"*Mama*, please stop it! You just don't know what happened, and every time I've tried to explain, you twist things all around."

"Well, okay, maybe I do," she said, "but let's be practical and realize that all those things happened to you a long time ago, *mijito*, and you're now a grown man with a wife and kids. Do you think your father and I could have succeeded in this country if we'd held onto all the bad things that happened to us? Oh, no, *mijito*, we all got to let go and keep going. That's our only hope," she said, making the sign of the cross over herself and adding the words, "*con el favor de Dios.*" Meaning, with the blessing of God.

"Yes, *Mama*, I can see that that's true," I said, taking in a deep breath, and I almost said 'but if this was really true, then why have you held onto so many bad things all these years?' But I didn't need to say this. It was my mother who now, looking at me in the eyes, said it best.

"And I also know, *mijito,* that I haven't always been a very good example of doing this," she said. "After all, it was your father, not me," she added, "who went to see Doctor Hoskins when he was sick and dying of cancer. I couldn't do that. In fact, enraged me that your father would do such a thing, because it had been that no good drunken doctor's fault that your brother Joseph died! Oh, he was the only doctor in town back then, and he caused so many deaths because of his stupid, drunken ways!"

She stopped and tears came to her eyes, and I took in another deep breath. I, too, remembered my brother's death very well. Joseph had been 16 years old and I'd been eight years old and he'd been my best friend. Oh, if he had lived I don't think that I would have flunked the third grade for a second time, because he'd always had a way of teaching me how to do things with such patience and good natural horse sense. In fact, he was the one who'd taught me how to play marbles and, with his teachings, I became the marble champion of my whole school.

"And yet looking back," continued my mother, "I'm beginning to now see how your father was able to do that, because, well, I'm approaching the end of my life, *mijito*, so I... I can now see that if we don't show forgiveness, then how can we expect God to show us forgiveness when we pass over?" And it was now my mother who took in a big, deep breath. "*Mijito*, you've got to go and see those nuns and priests," she added. "Truly, it will help you, yourself, deep inside of your heart and soul."

"Oh, *Mama*," I said.

"You say that they are old retired nuns and priests, right?"

"Yes," I said.

"Well, then, remember what happened to your little sister Teresita when the old dying nun asked to see her?"

"Remind me," I said.

"Well, they called me from Saint Mary's Star of the Sea and said that one of the nuns' old helpers was in the hospital dying and she wanted to see your little sister. I took Teresita, and the sick old woman called your sister to her bedside, but she refused to go near the old lady."

"How old was Sita at the time?" I asked. Most of us never called our youngest sister Teresita. We called her Sita for short and she liked it.

"She was about, well, I guess, maybe ten. And the woman begged her to come close, but you know how your sister is when she sets her mind to something."

My mother was absolutely right. Our little sister could be strong as iron. "Well, finally, the sick old woman said, 'Child, in the name of God, could you please forgive me for how I treated you all these years.'"

"I remember now," I said. "Sita shook her head, telling her no, that she would not forgive her, and she walked out of the room."

"Yes, exactly," said my mother, taking in another deep breath, "and I saw that old sick woman's face fill with fear, and all the nuns around her tried to console her, telling her that she'd been a very good person, but none of this helped. It was like, well, I guess, she was seeing hell itself deep inside of herself."

I nodded. "Yes, she probably was, *Mama*." And this was going to be tough, but I wasn't going to chicken out. "And do you remember who Sita was even more mad at than ... than at that old nun's helper?" I asked.

"No, tell me."

"You, *mama*," I said with tears bursting from my eyes. "You! Because during all those years of abuse you never once believed Sita! You always believed the nuns and that nun's old helper!"

"That's true," said my mother with tears also bursting from her eyes.

"Yeah, you'd thought that Sita had made it all up, just like you'd thought Linda and I had made up all our stuff about the nuns and priests."

"That's true, that's true," said my mother. "But how could I think differently? Those nuns would talk to your father and me with such respect and kindness, and ... and they'd dedicated their whole lives for the love of God and the good of humanity, so how could we believe that those same nuns and their helpers could be so abusive? It just didn't make sense, *mijito*."

"OH, *MAMA*," I yelled with my heart pounding, "AND THIS IS EXACTLY why I don't want to go to speak to those old nuns and priests! Am I just going to pretend that everything is Jim Dandy okay? Or am I going to be blunt and ask these old nuns and priests how many of them slapped kids, pulled their hair, and sneaked into the boys' bathroom, trying to see if they were touching themselves, so they could then scream at them that they were GOING TO GO TO HELL AND BURN FOR ETERNITY!

"Can't you understand, *Mama*, that it was no accident that these nuns and priests knew how to handle you guys? We, your kids, came into this world with Original Sin and all that crap, so we couldn't be trusted, and you, the adults, had your own daily ongoing sins, and so you couldn't trust yourselves, either, and so these nuns and priests had us all by the balls, trained to divide and conquer our *familia* just like armies divide and conquer nations. This is what Cortez did to México. His little group of soldiers could have never won if they hadn't been experts at manipulation and deception!

"Truly, I'm now beginning to realize that a lot of nuns and priests don't even believe in Jesus or in God. What they really believe in is … is the survival of their institution, and in keeping all the power in their own hands, so they can then accumulate huge amounts of wealth for their diocese and the Pope!"

"Oh, *mijito,* do you really believe this?"

"Absolutely! Look at all the gold they stole from the New World. And you, more than most people, should know this, because you were born in a gold mining town in México."

"But those were Americans who were taking the gold."

"Yes, but before the Americans it was Spain and the Church who raped all of the Americas! Let's not kid ourselves, *Mama,* it's been the Church who's been backing up the rich for centuries, so they can get their share of the spoils. Can't you see that, *mama?* You and *Papa* were adults and you were rich on top of that and … and … extremely generous with your donations, so of course, they spoke to you with respect and kindness. Truly, *Mama,* I just don't know how I can possibly go to see these old nuns and priests without WANTING TO RIP THEIR HEARTS OUT! And bluntly tell them what I really think of their manipulating, abusive ways?"

I stopped and took in a great big deep breath. "Oh, *Mama,*" I now said more gently, "I'll never forget how I climbed over that wall to go looking for my little nun and when I saw her sitting in the rose garden reading her Bible and I went up to her, she smiled at first, but then her whole face twisted into terror and she ran away from me in fear." The tears were streaming down my face. "What did they do to my beautiful, kind little nun, *Mama?* She must've been no more than eighteen years old, and she … she was the first teacher I ever had who was kind to me and didn't look down her nose at me when I didn't get it. Truly, I wish I'd bitten that smelly old mother superior's leg completely off!"

"*Mijito,* how can you talk like this?"

"Easy, *Mama,* easy," I said, wiping the tears off my face with the back of my hand, "it used to enrage me the way they'd always talk to you and *Papa.* They're all great actors. All the nuns and priests. And the best actors among them become the bishops and cardinals and mother superiors. I swear, they really got their pious little mannerisms down to a science. Remember how that old head nun out at the mission so quickly changed her whole way that first day when you slipped her that envelope full of money across the desk? Suddenly she couldn't do enough for us, and she became all smiles and told you that yes, of course, they'd be most happy to accept me and assign a nun to help teach me how to read after school.

"And then when that little young nun was so kind and nice to me that I fell in love with her and asked her if she would marry me when I got big, what did that old smelly nun do? She, who, I guess, had been outside of our door listening the whole time, came bursting into our room, slapped me across the face so hard that she knocked me out of my chair, called me the devil, and then she began slapping my little nun. And, *Mama,* Sister Theresa wouldn't fight back or even try to protect herself," I said with tears pouring down my face. "So this was when I leaped up off the floor and began biting the big old nun so she WOULDN'T KILL MY LOVING, KIND LITTLE NUN!" I added with a shout.

My mother was stunned. "But why didn't you tell us all this years ago? All we knew was that you'd bit a nun and they'd had to take her to the hospital."

"I tried, *Mama,*" I said. "I really tried to tell you, but I just couldn't find the words because I was a child, and they'd convinced me that I was evil and Mexican and sub- human. Truly, they were even worse to me than they'd been in public school when the teachers allowed the kids to keep making fun of me because I couldn't learn to read."

My mother reached into her pocket and brought out her hand embroidered handkerchief with the little pink flowers and green leaves, which she had embroidered while she and my dad watched T.V. together, and she handed it to me. I took the pretty little handkerchief and dried my eyes.

"Oh, *mijito*," she said, taking in a couple of great big, deep breaths, "it just seems to me that your father and I were so busy trying to be successful in this country that we failed as parents for you kids. Your older sister Tencha, just a young innocent girl and getting pregnant, or maybe even raped and having a child out of wedlock, and us being so ashamed and trying to keep up appearances that we quickly got her out of town and put her in a home down in San Diego where no one would know her. And then your brother, not liking football because he was so gentle, but still he played with all his heart so he, too, could fit in at school, and the coaches kept egging him on to keep playing until he injured himself. And then when we took him to see Dr. Hoskins, what did that no good drunk say, 'He only has growing pains, so keep him playing.'"

Tears came to my mother's eyes. "And your father and I could see that there was something very wrong with your brother, but we believed Dr. Hoskins because he was an American doctor, and we were too busy doing business to pay much attention. And it wasn't until the new young doctor named Pace came to town, who'd just gotten out of the Navy, that he took just one look at your brother and rushed him to Scripps Hospital in La Jolla. But it was too late. His football injuries had turned to yellow jaundice, injuries that could have been so easily taken care of at an earlier stage. Oh, we failed, *mijito!*" said my mother, with tears pouring down her face. "Your father and I, we failed all of you children!"

"Oh, *Mama*," I said, handing her back her embroidered handkerchief, "it's not you and *Papa* who failed. It's this whole system in which we live that has failed all of us."

"What do you mean?" she said, drying her eyes.

"Look, Doctor Hoskin's license should have been revoked years ago, *Mama,* and nuns and priests should never have been allowed and even encouraged to be abusive. You see, it's the very structure of these old out-of-date, male-based institutions that are failing us, the people, because they're full of secrecy, control, and have no real love and respect for ordinary people.

"Think about it, *Mama,* the very foundation of the Catholic Church is based on the… the concept of an all-male angry god who's full of wrath, and then we're told that we humans come into this world with Original Sin, so this then tells the Church to treat all of us as basically evil, and hence gives them the right to be abusive. Can you see that? It's an all male-based set up so that then a few old impotent men can… can manipulate all of us with ease. So, then, your failure wasn't your failure, *Mama.* You and *Papa* were always very wise good people, *Mama,* because both of you were raised by your Indigenous Indian mothers who were towers of faith and strength and believed in a kind, loving God who was both male and female."

"Well," she said, looking at me in a new way, "if this is what you really think, then maybe this is exactly what you should go and tell these retired nuns and priests."

"Are you kidding? This is what got me slapped until I was bloody out at the mission, *Mama*! Priests and nuns don't want to hear about any of this!"

"Yes, I'm sure that was true," she said. "But these nuns and priests have read your book, and so maybe they're minds have opened up."

"That would be a miracle," I said.

"Yes," she said, "and did we not raise you kids to understand that every day is, in fact, *otro milagro* given to us by God?"

I nodded. "Yes, that is how you raised us, *Mama,*" I said. "And this is also what I have been writing about all these years."

I stopped and breathed and my mother and I kept looking at each other. My dad had done this, too, and it was called eye gazing, which, according to Native People, was a Sacred Form of Heart to

Heart Soul Touching. I pushed back in my chair and got to my feet. I'd never expected to get into such a deep conversation with my mother. It was almost as if the Spirit of my dad had come into her now that he was on the Other Side of Living and she, too, had become a great talker.

"You're right, *Mama*," I said, "they have read *Rain of Gold*. That's why they've contacted me, so maybe they will be open for me to tell them what I really think and feel.

"But, oh, no, *Mama*," I added, shaking my head, "I don't know if I can do this! Not when I can't get it out of my head all the horrors that the Church has done! Hell, the Catholic Church alone, mostly through Spain and Portugal, slaughtered well over 60 to 80 million Native Americans in the name of God! And not just the men, but the women and children, too, like they slaughtered your mother's own Yaqui people, *Mama*! And damn it, nobody knows anything about this! Hell, what the Germans did to the Jews is small potatoes compared to what the Church has done worldwide! *Papa* knew this, and he wasn't afraid to admit it!"

"Yes," she said, with tears once more coming to her eyes, "and your father is also the one who found it in his heart to go and ... and forgive the man who was responsible for your brother's untimely death. He was only 16 years old," she added, "only 16, and still your father was able to forgive."

Hearing this, I now stopped all my talking and took my mother into my arms. I, too, remembered what my dad had done very well. I'd been about 17 years old and going to the Army Navy Academy in Carlsbad where my brother Joseph had also gone and that day I'd just gotten home from school when I found out that my dad had driven up California Street to see Dr. Hoskins. My mother had been screaming with rage and she'd demanded for me to get in our ranch truck and drive after my dad and stop him from seeing the doctor. But I hadn't wanted to get involved. Yet seeing my mother so angry, and she was normally such a calm person, I'd finally agreed to do what she asked and I'd gotten into our old ranch truck and drove after my dad.

And I'd gotten there just as my dad was walking past the corrals to where Dr. Hoskins was in his riding ring with one of his Tennessee Walkers. I'll never forget watching my dad in his big western hat walking up to the doctor in his English gear. Both of them were old, distinguished-looking grey-haired men. I watched the doctor dismount and take off his right-hand glove to shake my dad's hand.

Then I couldn't believe it. My dad was actually accepting the hand of the man who was responsible for my brother Joseph's death. I quickly turned to leave, but this was when my dad spotted me and waved me to come over so he could introduce me to this man that I'd avoided all of my life. I didn't know what to do, but my dad insisted and so I finally walked over, feeling like a traitor to my brother and mother.

"This is our other son, Edmundo," said my dad. My parents always called me by my middle name Edmundo at home.

My eyes flashed with rage and the doctor saw it, but still he reached out to take my hand. And what did I do? I couldn't believe it, I, too, reached out and took his hand, but if he had so much as squeezed my hand just a little bit, I would've jerked him to me and side stepped him, slamming him to the ground as we did at our wrestling workouts every afternoon at the Academy. But he didn't squeeze my hand like a lot of old men do trying to show that they still have power. No, he shook my hand with such gentleness that in his own way he was saying he … he was sorry. So I didn't slam him, but still I quickly took my hand back and just stood there listening. And my dad and the old doctor spoke about horses and the price of hay and not one single word was ever mentioned about my brother. And yet before my dad and I left, I could see in both of these old men's eyes that a peace had been made between them, and that the doctor, who was now himself dying of cancer, was truly grateful that my dad had come to see him. I took in several deep breaths, remembering all this.

"Okay, *Mama*," I finally said, "maybe you're right, and I should go and see these old retired nuns and priests. But truly, I don't know what I'll do when I get there."

"You will pray, *mijito,* you will pray and ask God for guidance, and then you will know what to do, and who knows, this ... this might end up being the most important talk of your life."

"What? Why would you say this, *Mama?*"

"Because, *mijito,* over and over again your father and I found in business here in the United States, that that which we really didn't want to do was often the very thing that caused us to learn the most and grow the most."

"Well, yes, but this isn't business."

"Oh, isn't the business of religion the biggest business in all the world? You, yourself, spoke of this only moments ago."

I nodded. "Yes, I guess you're right."

"Look, *mijito,* your father never wanted to stop bootlegging, but then when he was forced to stop because prohibition was over and we got that pool hall from Archie in Carlsbad and we went legal, our whole life changed in a way that we'd never dreamed possible. Doors that had been previously closed to us suddenly opened up. It was like now that we were business people, the *Americanos* no longer saw us as *Mejicanos,* but instead as other business people. It was like a miracle, I tell you, so you now go and see these nuns and priests and do not be surprised that—with the help of Our Sacred Blessed Mother and Her Son Jesus—that this might end up ... not just being the most important talk of your life, but also a whole new miraculous change of life for you here in your heart, *con el favor de Dios,*" she added, making the sign of the cross and then kissing the back of her right thumb which she'd placed over her index finger, making a cross.

"Oh, *Mama,*" I said.

"Eh, don't you 'oh, Mama' me," she said. "You pray tonight, *mijito,* you pray and ask Our Lord Jesus to teach you how to find it in your heart to forgive just as He did on the cross and how your father was also able to do with Hoskins. And I'm not saying th--
this is easy, *mijito,* because only now that I'm appro
few years am I finally beginning to understand wha
really all about."

18

"And what's that, *Mama*?"

"Forgiveness, *mijito*," she said, "I'm now beginning to see is...is the only way for we mortals can find peace in our hearts." She stopped and took in a big breath. "So I can now see that your father...was absolutely right that day he went to see that no good doctor, but I just couldn't see it back then, and...and, well, sometimes I still have trouble seeing it even today."

It was me who now took in a big, deep breath and blew out fast. This was a big one for my mother. Maybe even the biggest. Yes, my mother was showing a lot of guts to admit this.

"Me, too, *Mama*," I now said, "me, too. Oh, that little nun! Do you realize that every woman I've ever been attracted to since then has had some kind of likeness to my little nun? AND THEY DESTROYED HER, *MAMA!*" I yelled. "THEY REALLY DID!"

But my mother didn't panic or get flustered by my outburst and simply said, "Well, then, *mijito*, maybe this is exactly what you're supposed to speak about to these old nuns and priests. Remember, they, too, were young once and...and maybe they, too, were destroyed, and this is why they got mean."

I nodded, and nodded again. Maybe what my mother was saying was right. After all, all through my writing I always wrote—like Anne Frank had so well written in her diary—that no matter what, she still believed that people were basically good of heart.

"Okay, *Mama*," I said. "I'll pray, I really will, and I'll ask for guidance, and then I'll go see them. Thank you. You've really been a big help. Thank you very much."

"I'm glad I was able to help you, *mijito*, because...as you well know...I've never been a very good talker like your father and his mother. Oh, how that little skinny Indian woman could talk. I swear, the birds would come out of the sky to hear her speak," she added with laughter.

And so we hugged in a big *abrazo*, and then I went back across the grass and the chicken coops to the big old house that was so rundown that my parents had been very smart to want to move into the nice new smaller house. I could hear the goats and the horses in the distance and, of course, the chickens when I went inside to collect the eggs. I was feeling pretty good now. I was no longer all-divided and confused inside. No, I was now centered, and the teaching of my Native American *mamagrandes*—through *mi mama*—had done it once again. After all, when it was all said and done, we, Human People, really were like the weeds, as my dad's mother *Doña Margarita*, always said, "indestructible as we reached for the Light of God!"

TWO

O h, i'd always loved flying!
     In high school my best friend, John Folting, got his pilot's license when he was 16 years old and he immediately took me up in a little propeller powered plane that had no doors and flew so slowly that the cars below us would go past us. We flew just a few hundred feet above the earth, and the land below us became alive with jackrabbits in the valleys, quail in the canyons, and deer on the mesas. Oh, seeing the world from a bird's point of view was spectacular and totally all new to me. Then I'll never forget, up ahead I saw that we were approaching some green meadows and little ponds and this was when I saw a waterfall that I'd never known even existed in San Diego County, but John then banked the little plane and we headed back.

"NO!" I shouted over the noise of the propeller. "Let's keep going! I want to see that waterfall and those meadows and little ponds!"

"WE CAN'T!" he yelled back at me. "That's México! We can't cross international borders without advance notice and approval!"

"What border?" I shouted. "I don't see any border! That's the same kind of brush and oak trees and rocky hills as we've got here all around us!"

I'll never forget, John started laughing and laughing. "What did you expect to see, a concrete wall like they have in China?"

"Well, no," I said, feeling all embarrassed, "but I guess I did expect to at least see something."

That day I was totally shocked to find out that... that in reality the world was borderless, and so incredibly beautiful and full of natural abundance, and now here I was aboard a huge commercial jet and once again looking out my window as we flew across the western United States. And once more I could see that our whole Mother Earth was so fantastic and beautiful and full of abundance as I flew northeast from San Diego, California to the city of Minneapolis at the border of Minnesota and Wisconsin. And yet I could still not see any visual borders. No, everything just worked together in unity and color. First came the rocky brush covered hills of Southern California that looked like they were covered with fur and a few trees in the canyons, then came the huge valleys of agriculture with those great big green circles—so easy to irrigate because it only took one huge turning sprinkler on monstrous wheels per circle—and then there were also long straight rows of orchards stretching out for miles, and then all of this was surrounded by vast deserts painted in colors of orange and red and white with veins of blue.

Then when I thought I couldn't take in another ounce of beauty, here came the sculptured Grand Canyon with all its wonder and majesty, then, of course, next came the tall snow-capped Rocky Mountains. Oh, I was once more in love, taking in Beauty with a capital 'B' as my *mamagrande* had always taught me how to do. In fact, I'd forgotten that I was going to see old retired nuns and priests until we landed, and then it all came rushing back into me. And even though I'd prayed and asked for guidance as my mother had suggested, I still had no real idea why I'd really accepted this speaking engagement.

At the airport a man dressed in a dark suit had a sign with my name on it. I hadn't expected this. Usually when I spoke at high schools and universities, I was picked up by the teachers or professors. This was really pretty extravagant. These old nuns and priests were really putting on a show for me. The man immediately took my luggage and took me out to a long black car, put my bag in the trunk, and then quickly opened the back door of the limousine for me. I almost laughed. This really wasn't my style.

"And in a little cooler you'll find water and beer and wine and some snacks that were prepared for you," he said. "You see, we'll be taking a two hour drive from the city of Minneapolis out into the country."

"Thank you," I said, and I slipped off my small day backpack and got into the back of the big luxurious car.

Normally I liked to sit up front with the driver and visit when I came to a new place, but this time I didn't want to talk to anyone. No, I had to gather myself. My mother's words had truly gotten deep inside of me. If she was right and this was going to maybe end up being the most important talk of my life, then I still had some heavy soul searching to do.

I took in a deep breath. Ever since I'd had my talk with my mother, it also seemed like I just couldn't get Sister Theresa out of my mind. Yes, I'd only been an eight year old, and yet I'd never quit loving that kind, soft-spoken little nun. How could I? Something deep inside of me had known, within the first moment I met her, that she'd been meant to be the love of my life.

Breathing deeply, I looked out the window of the big dark car as we drove away from the airport. I could see that there was a little snow on the ground and most of the trees had lost their leaves. Then we were out of the city and traveling across farm land with large barns, then we were travelling alongside a huge lake, and I could see that all this terrain was mostly flat and wooded, a very different type of terrain than the dry, rugged, wide-open western United States that I was used to. But still I also found it to be just as breathtakingly beautiful as the land that we'd flown over.

Oh, looking out at the huge lake with its tiny splashing waves, I wished that I'd really come to go fishing so I could get to know the local people and we could talk about what kind of fish they caught and what did they do to keep their lake so clean and beautiful. A large part of me still wished that ... that I really hadn't come to see some old retired nuns and priests.

I mean, yeah, sure, my mother had explained to me that forgiveness was our only hope, and I agreed with her, but also I had to admit that forgiveness had never been my style. After all, I wasn't my brother Joseph who'd always been so kind and gentle. I was Cain. Not Abel. In fact, at my first public talk back in 1973 when my first book *MACHO!* had come out, and the keynote speaker, a famous author, was too drunk to do the keynote, so it ended up that I spoke to the 500 teachers of English in Long Beach, California, and believe me, I'd shown no forgiveness.

Sure, I'd had notes, and I'd been prepared to give a nice little talk about all the research and interviewing that I'd had to do to write *MACHO!* but then when I'd looked out at that sea of white teachers' faces and I hadn't seen one Black, Asian, or Mexican face, my heart EXPLODED and I'd tossed my notes away, pulled down my Stetson, and I'd gone for the jugular.

"I understand you're all English teachers," I'd said with a huge booming voice.

They'd laughed, thinking that this was a compliment.

"Well," I'd continued, "I'd like you all to know that I once had an English teacher, and … and I hope that that English teacher dies a painful death that lasts at least a week! BECAUSE!" I'd screamed, "I can forgive bad parents because maybe it was an accident, and they didn't even want to be parents, BUT ENGLISH TEACHERS ARE NO ACCIDENT!" I'd yelled. "You guys study to become teachers! You study for years, and so no, I will not forgive you English teachers who are abusive and torture kids with commas and periods and misspelling, making them feel like less than human, because they can't seem to be able to GET IT RIGHT!"

My publisher's representative, a woman from back east who was standing to the right of me behind the stage curtains, went bonkers and came rushing towards me to get me off the stage. But I'd turned and yelled at her, too.

"GET BACK AWAY FROM ME! I will not be silenced! These teachers came to hear a writer speak, AND THEY WILL NOW HEAR A WRITER SPEAK!"

And with that conviction, I continued with my foot to the pedal, and told the 500 English teachers that, on the other hand,

I prayed to God with all my heart and soul for teachers who were patient, attentive, considerate, and kind, that these would go to Heaven when they passed and they'd be rewarded with apple pie and vanilla ice cream for all of eternity.

Tears had started pouring down my face and my publisher's representative began shitting square bricks, but then to her shock, when at the end of my talk I received a standing ovation that lasted for several minutes, she quickly changed her position, acting like the whole thing had been her idea. And my book *Macho!* became a west coast bestseller, and it was reviewed by the L.A. Times and compared to the best of John Steinbeck.

So, well, then, maybe, my mother was wrong and it wasn't about forgiveness and I should just go straight for the jugular with these nuns and priests, too. I mean, that time back in 1973, I'd just gone for it with all my heart and soul and so maybe I should do the same thing again.

Hell, this was also how I'd become a writer.

I'd just gone for it with all my heart and soul come hell or high water! The year was 1960. I was 19 years old and I'd just come back from México to the U.S. three days before, and all those old hor- rible racist feelings that I'd had growing up with since kindergarten had come EXPLODING back up inside of me, but, well, that was also another story, so I won't go into that right now.

Anyway, these were the kind of memories that were going through my head until I got hungry and reached for the little cooler that was by my feet alongside my one day backpack, and I saw that there was a pretty pink little bag attached to the cooler. I took the pretty little bag in hand and opened it and there was a red rose inside with a note.

Instantly a smile came to my face. Who would have ever thought? I took the rose in hand and smelled of it and it smelled of Heaven, and then I read the note. It was handwritten in beautiful penmanship and simply said, "Please enjoy your drive alongside our beautiful lake, and you'll find that your pastrami sandwich has extra hot mustard just like you like it." And there was no signature. Just a little hand-drawn heart with the word "love" below it.

I was stunned.

What was this all about? And how had they found out that I liked pastrami with extra hot mustard? Then when I got a beer out of the cooler, it was a Stella, my favorite, along with Modelo and Pacifico. Had these old nuns and priests spoken with my mother or with my wife Barbara? I couldn't stop smiling as I ate my thick, delicious pastrami and drank down both beers. I was sound asleep when we drove up to the huge retirement home. Waking up, I took in several deep breaths, centering myself, and glanced around. This retirement home was a great big old beautiful mansion built on a knoll over-looking the large expanse of water that we'd been following. There were Canadian Honkers on the grass and the well-maintained grass rolled all the way down to the water's edge.

I breathed again and again.

My mother had been absolutely right, there were no accidents and I wasn't a kid anymore. I was now an adult. A published author. And so if I couldn't get past my own crap, then how could I ever expect for others to get past theirs? The buck had to stop here. My God, a rose, and then a pastrami with lots of hot mustard and a Stella, the oldest beer I knew of, started in 1366.

Yeah, sure, no doubt about it, it was me who had to change my…thinking, because the change we wanted for the world had to start within each of us, here deep inside of our own Hearts and Souls. Not over there with abusive nuns and priests and teachers, but right here within me, you, all of us. I got out of the car. I didn't want the driver to open the door for me. I really didn't like all that subservient crap, especially when I was dressed in old worn out Levis, cowboy boots, western hat, and a beat-up sheepskin jacket. An elderly man came out to greet me. He was smiling and in regular street clothes, but still I guessed he was a priest.

"Hello," he said, with a voice full of joy. "We're so happy you accepted our invitation." He laughed. "A few of us were getting a little worried that you might not come, because of the interviews you've done and you mentioned all those abusive things that happened to you at Catholic school. Father James," he added, sticking out his hand with a big smile.

I took his hand. "Well, you guys were right," I said. "I almost didn't come. It was my mother who talked me into coming."

"Well, then, we need to thank your mother. Lupe, correct?"

I nodded. "Yes, Lupe."

"A beautiful woman," continued Father James. "Here, let me help you with your backpack. You've had a long trip."

"No, thank you," I said. "I always like to keep my pack in my own hands at all times."

"Oh," he said, as the three of us went up the stairs. And it was one at the most deliberate "oh's" I'd ever heard.

"My God, this place is beautiful," I said once we were inside.

And I meant it. The whole backside was made up of tall magnificent windows that looked out on the rolling hill of green grass and the large expanse of water. I walked up to the windows. There were two nice big fat whitetail deer just beyond the Canadian honkers by the water's edge.

"Wow! What a gorgeous place! The deer, the honkers, the natural grass, and this huge body of water that looks like a whole entire sea! Truly, a land of plenty! Is this Lake Michigan?"

"No, it's Lake Superior."

"Really? I thought Lake Michigan was the big one."

He smiled. "All five Great Lakes are very large," he said.

"Oh, and this structure, who built it?" I asked. "The fine woodwork, the window panes, the arches, the marble floors. What great expansive architecture."

"I'm glad you appreciate it," he said with a big smile. "You see, at the turn of last century this was built as a hunting lodge by a few very rich powerful men, who liked to get together now and then, so they could make some of the major decisions for our country."

"Really? For our entire nation, eh?"

"Yes, and they had barges of material brought in from Europe and floated across the lake to this remote location so they could meet in total privacy."

I started laughing.

"What is it?" he asked.

"So those tough, greedy old conniving so-and-so's finally began to fear death, and decided to give the whole place to you guys for insurance for their souls, eh?" I said, cracking up with *carcajadas*, meaning big belly shaking laughter.

"Well," he said, "I hadn't quite thought of it like that, but you might be right. Come this way," he added. "You have time to go to your room and rest before dinner, which will be very simple, then you can get a good night's rest for tomorrow's events. I hope you don't mind, but we've invited some outside teachers and administrators to join our activities."

"No, of course not," I said. "The more, the merrier!"

"Good," he said. "After reading your books, I told them that you wouldn't be intimidated."

"Which of my books have you read?"

"*Macho, Jury*, and of course, your most fabulous book, *Rain of Gold*. But I must say, I do believe that in some ways *Jury* might just be my favorite. Did Naomi really change her vote to guilty because of cat food?"

Jury was the true story of the minute-by-minute deliberations of the Juan Corona murder trial, the largest mass murder ever committed in the United States at that time.

I laughed. "Yes, she really did, and it shocked people when Juan Corona was convicted because Hawk, the defense attorney, had torn the prosecution case apart."

"So I read," he said, "but the foreman, Ernie Phillips, guided the jurors with such, well, honesty and simplicity that they all finally voted for guilty except for Naomi."

"Exactly," I said.

"But then Naomi's sister called her and told her she was leaving, that she was going back to her own home, and her cats were out of food. I couldn't put the book down, because this then told me that the whole course of history can be changed by the most trivial and meaningless of reasons."

"Yes, but also the right decision was made by the jurors," I said, taking in a deep breath, "because after the trial ... well, Juan Corona's priest came to me and he talked, but, of course, I can never write about what he told me."

"Really"

"Yes."

"Oh, if I'm guessing correctly it must've been haunting his soul," said Father James, also taking in a deep breath.

"Amen," I said. "Truly, I learned a lot by doing *Macho* and *Jury*. In fact, I'm sure I could have never done *Rain* if I hadn't done those two books first."

"I can now understand that very well," he said. "*Rain of Gold* is an incredible work," he added.

"Really, you think so?" I said.

"Absolutely," he said, "I've read it three times already, and I've never done that with any other book, except, of course, for the Bible."

Hearing this, I took in a deep breath. Maybe these nuns and priests had really opened up, and so maybe, just maybe, they weren't going to panic if I told them what I really thought about the Roman Catholic Church.

"Well, I'm very glad to hear this," I said to Father James, "because, you see, I quit on *Rain of Gold* many times. I'd just get all full of doubt, and the years would pass, but then I'd re-interview my parents and give it another try. I swear, the truth is that I didn't have the talent or brains with which to pull *Rain* off, and yet, each time I'd go back to it, it was like I now had, well, new insights and ... and a deeper understanding what it was that my parents were really telling me." I laughed. "Both my dad and mom got so frustrated with me a few times that they told me I'd just become so *gringo*-ized that I was constipated in the brain and so I could never understand the world that my two Native American *mamagrandes* had come from, but I just kept trying and trying."

"Well, we're all very glad you did," he said, "because the book shows that it was inspired by God."

"Really? You think the book shows that? I mean, it took me 16 years to write *Rain* and by the time I turned it in to my New York publisher, Marc Jaffe, and all the other people I'd known at Bantam-Random House were no longer there, or had died."

"Well, I can tell you that we've all read *Rain of Gold* and we're very happy you didn't quit and completed the book," he said. "But I also I believe that we should save the rest of this conversation for the others. So now please let me just take you to your room."

"Sure, of course." I said.

And as we walked further into the grand great-looking old place, I didn't see any people anywhere. The whole place seemed deserted.

"Where is everyone?" I asked.

"At chapel, or in their rooms."

"Oh," I said, and it was now my turn to give a very deliberate 'oh.' I'd been so caught up in the grandeur of the place and talking about *Rain* that I'd almost forgotten to whom it was that I'd be speaking.

My room was on the second story and was large and beautiful with a balcony overlooking the lake. There were now four deer on the grassy area by the water's edge and another big bunch of honkers had flown in. There were now about 200 birds. I'd never been in a natural setting of such beauty and abundance. It reminded me a lot of Yosemite, California, and the famous world class Ahwanee Lodge.

I unpacked, then decided to lie down to rest for a few minutes. It was a good comfortable bed. Firm but not too firm. And I guess that, well, I fell into a deep sleep, because the next thing I knew, I awoke and it was dark and yet there was some light coming from the far end of my room. I got up on my elbows and saw that a man was standing across the room from me and a bright and yet soft golden light surrounded him.

I rubbed my eyes, thinking that I was still asleep and dreaming all this, but then I realized I was awake and breathing fast, and the man was now gone. And for the life of me, I couldn't remember where I was. So I lay back down and, little by little, I began to remember that I was at a retirement home of old nuns and priests by Lake Superior and not Lake Michigan. And that the last time I'd had a man come to me surrounded by a bright and yet soft golden light had been in Madrid, Spain and ... and that man had been Our Lord Jesus Christ.

I sat up, took in a deep breath, and blew out fast. And back then in Spain, when Jesus had come to me, made total sense, because I'd been completely Open of Heart and ... and my *familia* and I and a group of Native Americans had gone to Spain in the name of worldwide harmony and peace and abundance for all, and so what was I now being told by Jesus? Was I now being told that forgiveness wasn't enough, but that I also had to have a completely Open Heart*Corazon* for these nuns and priests?

Oh, my God! I got up and went to the restroom, took a long pee, then washed my hands and face. At times like this I sometimes felt like I was crazy*loco*. Who did I think I was to really think that Jesus had come to in Spain and then here in Wisconsin once again? But then, as I continued washing my face with cold water and my *mamagrandes'* teaching began coming back to me and I once more realized that there really was no separation between us and the Spirit World once we let go and we started seeing with our HeartEyes and not just our HeadEyes, then yes, of course, Jesus had just come to me now as He'd come to me in Spain and ... and as He'd come to me the first time just north of Buccaneer Beach in South Oceanside when I'd been eight years old.

I smiled, remembering that beautiful day when I'd been eight years old.

Joseph, my brother and best friend, had just passed over a few days before, and I'd suddenly been awakened right before daybreak and told in no uncertain terms that I was supposed to go to the corrals and saddle up my brother's horse Midnight Duke.

I got up, slipped on my Levis and boots, and quickly went out to the corrals and Duke came walking up to me out of the dark as if he, too, had been told that we were supposed to do something very important. And that day a miracle happened After saddling up the big all black horse, I pushed him against a fence so I mount up, and then I turned inland, figuring that we were supposed to go up our valley towards the new cemetery where my brother Joseph was buried. But no, Duke refused to go that way and he turned going down our valley towards Buccaneer Beach at the west end of our ranch.

The Father Sun had just begun illuminating the world with beautiful colors of yellow and orange when we got to the beach, and suddenly Midnight Duke began calling out to sea with great big belly expanding screeches that spread my little short legs apart, and then with another great powerful screech, he leaped into the big rolling waves. I'd been terror-stricken. I didn't know how to swim, then these fins came in all around us and I'd thought they were sharks and they were going to tear us apart.

But Duke wasn't frightened and began talking to them in little bird-like chirping sounds that I didn't know horses could make and they made chirping sounds back to Duke. This was when I realized that they were dolphins, and Duke turned his head to the left and I saw that he'd spotted my brother Joseph walking on water along-side Our Lord Jesus just beyond a big black rock and the break-ers. Duke was so happy to see my brother whom he'd always love so much. I'll never forget, a great joy came into me and I felt so blessed that I made the sign of the cross over myself and I now understood that when one of our loved ones passed over, we weren't losing them. No, we were gaining an even closer relationship with Our Lord Jesus.

And now remembering all this so vividly, brought a smile to my face and I looked in the mirror above the sink, and instantly I caught a quick flash of Jesus being behind me, and He, too, was smiling.

"Hi," I said into the mirror.

"Hello," he said from the mirror.

"Thanks for coming with me," I said.

And saying this, I began laughing and laughing with big *car-cajadas*. What a ridiculous thing to say, there were no boundaries of Space and Time for Jesus, and once we accepted Him, then, of course, there were no boundaries of Space and Time for us, and so He was always with us. It wasn't like He would have stayed behind in California and I'd come to Wisconsin by myself. And He now started laughing and laughing, too, and it felt so good. Yeah, sure, of course, it wasn't bad for me to be crazy*loco*. Hell—I mean Heaven—there was really no other way to live, except being crazy-*loco* full of Love*Amor!* After all, Life, *la Vida*, was a VoyageDream and maybe it was Confucius who had said it best:

Row, row, row your boat,
Gently down the stream,
Merrily, merrily, merrily,
Life is but a dream!

Oh, I was suddenly feeling so happy! BIG BIG HAPPY! Feeling the Presence of Jesus always felt so good, I just couldn't stop smiling. I slipped on my Levis, and went across the room to the balcony to look up at the stars. But opening the balcony door, the freezing cold hit me like a wall of ice. I quickly closed the door.

Shivering, I went across the room and got back in bed under the big warm comforter. And as I lay in bed, I began to realize that Jesus was always really, really, really with me, with you, with all of us when we were Open of Heart like I'd been in Spain and He'd come to endorse our movement of Snow Goose Global Thanksgiving, meaning that we were taking our greatest U.S. celebration of Thanksgiving, when Native Americans and Europeans ate in harmony and peace together, and going global with it. And so Jesus had now come to me again, because He was endorsing this talk I was going to have with these old retired nuns and priests.

Tears came to my eyes. Yes, of course, this was it, but I just hadn't seen it, because once more I was such a Doubting Thomas. OH, WHEN WAS I EVER GOING TO LEARN?!?

I breathed.

I breathed again and again and I guess that I went back to sleep, because the next thing I knew, I awoke and there was sunlight coming in my window. Why, I'd slept the whole night through. The whole eastern sky was now painted in gorgeous colors of red and orange and pink with spectacular streaks of dazzling blue and soft purple. I took in several deep breaths, blew out fast, got up, found I was still wearing my Levis, and crossed the room to step out on the balcony, and to my surprise, the cold didn't hit me like a wall of ice this time. No, it was like the cold now embraced me with a crisp, good feeling of energizing Love*Amor*.

I laughed.

I smiled. It felt so invigorating that I quickly put both of my hands over my heart, and began giving greetings to the Father Sun as I'd been doing ever since I began to write on the 16th of September 1960 at 6 a.m. back home on the *rancho* in South Oceanside at the north end of Stewart Street.

"GOOD MORNING! GOOD MORNING! GOOD MORNING, FATHER SUN!" I shouted, pounding my heart area with both of my open hands and looking out at the Sun, the Right Eye of God.

"FROM MY HEART!" I shouted again, pounding again. "Good morning, Father Sun! Goodnight, Mother Moon," who was, of course, the Left Eye of God. "*Con todo mi corazón*, good morning, good morning, Father Sky, Mother Earth, and All Our Holy Stars, *nuestra familia!* Our great great grandparents and aunts and uncles! All of Our Ancestry who've already come here to *Tierra Santa* and completed their Holy Work for the Almighty and His/Her ongoing Sacred Garden of Heaven on Mother Earth!

"FROM MY HEART, GOOD MORNING! GOOD MORNING!" I shouted even louder, giving Love*Amor* with all my Heart and Soul to the whole entire Universe! "Good morning, *familia!* Good morning! Good morning! GOOD MORNING!"

And I now began laughing with *carcajadas!*

Oh, it felt so good down deep inside to be doing this Sacred Holy Ritual of giving thanks that my *mamagrande* had taught to do when I'd been a child and I'd been performing every single day since then, giving thanks to the Almighty for His/Her precious gift of *otro milagro!*

I breathed and breathed and glanced around and saw that the honkers were already up and munching, like an army of great big birds, bobbing their heads up and down in a quick singing rhythm as they ate the tips off the grass. And the lake waters were shimmering and splashing and the trees were also singing in the breeze. Oh, it was a symphony of life and sound and color, and then two white tail deer suddenly came prancing by with their ears pointing forward and highly alert.

Something must've startled them, and then I saw them, Five Native Americans, dressed in buckskin and fur, and they were walking about three feet above the ground just like Jesus had hovered about two feet above the floor when He'd come to me this morning and when He'd come to me in Spain. I called out, waving to my Five Native Brothers, and they turned and waved back to me, then they, too, ShapeShifted out of this Dimension and into another just as Jesus had also done so easily.

THREE

So I went back inside, did my floor exercises, showered, dressed, and went down for breakfast. I was starving. In the lobby, I saw people going to a room to the right just off of the huge, beautiful main dining room. I followed them, thinking they might lead me to food. There were about 30 people in the smaller room. They were all elderly and dressed in street clothes and most of them were women. The men, who were very few, were all over by the food which was set out on two long white linen covered tables by the large expanse of windows overlooking the grass and the lake.

I could now see that it had been a good thing that I'd slept through the whole night and I hadn't met any of these people for dinner last night, because, well, I'm sure that if I'd met them last night, I would have probably just been looking at them and trying to figure out which nun had been the meanest and which priest had been the child molester. But now that I'd slept the whole night through and Jesus had come to me as He'd done in Madrid, Spain, I was seeing things very differently. Simply, I was seeing these nuns and priests as just happy looking old people.

Father James was the first one to come up to me. "Good morning," he said with a great big smile. "How did you sleep?"

"Very well, thank you," I said. "How about you? How did you sleep?" "Not so good. It's hard to sleep at my age."

"Oh, how old are you?"

"I'm going on 82," he said.

"My dad was older than you and every night he slept like a baby," I said. "Well, I wish I knew his secret," he said, laughing. "In fact, I bet many of us would like to know."

And I almost said, "Well, maybe my dad slept like a baby because he had a clear conscious and a lot of you guys don't." But I didn't say this, and instead just kept quiet. After all, I had to keep an Open Heart as Jesus had let me know, especially if I hoped to accomplish anything worthwhile with all these old nuns and priests.

"I'll be introducing you," he continued. "Is there anything special that you'd like me to say?"

"No, not really. Just go for it, but please keep it short, okay?"

"Of course," he said.

Then he walked me over to the two tables where the food was laid out.

"As you can see," he said, "we mostly have rolls and coffee and fruit, but there are also eggs and bacon available. You never came down for dinner last night, did you?" he added.

"No, I didn't," I said, "and I'm starving, so yes, I'd really like to have a big full breakfast." I laughed. "I had such vivid wonderful dreams I awoke laughing!"

"Really? You awoke laughing?"

"Yes, and it was wonderful!"

"I'll be," he said. "Maybe it's hereditary. Your grandmother, *Doña Margarita*—I hope I pronounced it right—if I'm not mistaken, awoke laughing many times, too."

"Yes, you pronounced very well, and you're right. My grandmother would explain to us that when we sleep, our Guardian Angel takes us back up to Heaven to sleep in the Holy Arms of *Papito Dios*, so how can we not awake laughing, eh?"

"Well, maybe this is something you can tell us all about, too," he said. "You see, this is what many of us found so fascinating about your book. It was almost like your grandmothers didn't worship God, but instead—how can I say this—they lived with God."

"Exactly, because in many native languagings, breathing and God are the exact same word."

"Really? Oh, you will definitely need to tell us about this!"

"I'll be glad to," I said.

Wow, I was really beginning to see that it was a Godsend that I'd come. What a waste it had been for me to carry around inside of me all this hate and rage for nuns and priests all these years. But, well, on the other hand, maybe it hadn't been a waste, because my rage and hate had also been part of my main driving force through all those years of rejection.

Father James had them prepare two eggs and four crisp pieces of bacon for me and also a mountain of country potatoes, and a couple of slices of rye toast with butter and strawberry jam on the side. I ate everything and drank down two full cups of my own Yogi herbal tea that I always carried with me in my backpack, and now I was ready.

Most people had taken their seats, and I could see that almost everyone had a copy of *Rain of Gold,* and a few also had *Macho!* and *Jury.* My next two books, that would complete the trilogy of *Rain of Gold, Thirteen Senses* and *Wild Steps of Heaven,* wouldn't be out for another year.

Father James and a very handsome young-looking man were making a final check of the microphone. I took in a deep breath and walked across the room in my western boots over towards the podium that was by the large expanse of windows. Glancing out, I saw that the whitetail deer were gone, but most of the Canadian honkers were still grazing on the grass outside the huge windows. Other honkers were lying down and resting. I smiled. Oh, I just loved this beautiful natural setting!

Then Father James called people to order and did my introduction, but he didn't keep it short like he'd agreed to do. Instead he did like a lot of teachers and professors did and he praised my work, my talent, and especially my tenacity of having endured over 265 rejections from New York publishers. And then he still didn't stop and he went on to say how my first book *Macho!* was immediately compared to the best of John Steinbeck by the *Los Angeles Times.* This always embarrassed me to no end, because, in my opinion,

John Steinbeck—and not Hemingway or Fitzgerald—had to be the best writer of our country, truly giving voice to the real people of our nation. And then to further embarrass me, he added that it was an honor I'd come to be with them.

"In fact, he almost didn't accept our invitation until his mother Lupe convinced him to come," he added with laughter.

After receiving some applause and cheering, I walked over to Father James and gave him a big hug, and at first he resisted, but then relaxed and hugged me back. I thanked him and stepped up to the podium as he walked over and took a seat along with the priests who were all in the back.

"Thank you," I said. "Thank you very much, and the honor is really mine to be here. And I loved that red rose and the note and that thick wonderful pastrami with lots of extra hot mustard that you guys put in the little cooler for me in the limo."

The faces of the nuns directly in front of me lit up with joy. I smiled and nodded to them, and they all smiled and nodded back, except for one cute little short nun with grey curly hair who turned all red with embarrassment, and quickly glanced away. Oh, then this maybe meant that the others didn't know about the flower and the note.

I laughed and glanced around. All the nuns were in the first three rows, and the priests were all behind them, and some of these hadn't even taken their seats yet. I closed my eyes. I wasn't going to let this bother me, so I just took in a deep breath, gathering myself deep inside, then ... then I realized that I had absolutely no idea where to begin. I'd never spoken to a roomful of nuns and priests before. I usually spoke to teachers, professors, students, law enforcement groups, and/or other community organizations.

I kept my eyes closed and asked for guidance, and it came to me to start out with a story, and maybe even the story of my nephew Erik and how I'd taken him to the beach one day. Yes, yes, especially if I concluded about the incoming and outgoing waves being like our Mother Earth's 26,000 year cycle of male and female global energy. Then after I accomplished this, I would then ask them to please join me in a Native American prayer that I'd learned a few years back, and by doing these two things, then I'd have a better feel of where I could go with these nuns and priests without losing them.

"GOOD MORNING!" I said in a loud happy voice. "Good morning! Good morning! Good morning! How did you all sleep? Good, I hope. Myself, I slept like a baby and awoke smiling and laughing, then I when out on my balcony and I saw the Father Sun, the Right Eye of God, coming up with all His splendor and wonder, which, according to my two Indian *mamagrandes* makes every day *otro milagro de Dios*, another Miracle straight from God, as you already know since... since you've read *Rain of Gold*."

I stopped. My heart was pounding. Something was happening to me deep inside. I just couldn't start out with a little story. No, first I'd have to bluntly tell them why it was that I almost hadn't accepted this speaking engagement.

"But now," I said, "before I can begin my talk with the little story of taking my nephew Erik to the beach one day or... or even ask you to share with me why you invited me to come to see you, I first need to let all of you know that Father James was right, and I almost didn't accept this speaking engagement, because... because of all the abuse I received at the hands of nuns and priests as a young boy."

Tears came to my eyes and I took in several deep breaths and I could well see that I'd definitely surprised them and a few even looked like they were ready to bolt.

"But please bear with me," I said, closing my eyes, "because, you see, it's going to, well, turn out for the good." I opened my eyes and blew out fast. "After days of procrastination, I went to see my mother and we had a *quesadilla* with homemade *salsa* and avocado, and she, who you all know as Lupe in the book and is now almost 90 years old, told me in no uncertain terms that I had to find forgiveness in my heart just as Our Lord Jesus had done on the cross, and come and see all of you because this could very well end up being the most important talk of my life."

The tears were now running down my face. "Look, I was eight years old when I fell in love with the little young nun who was teaching me how to read after school in the fourth grade." I wiped the tears off my face. "She was so kind to me. In fact, she was my first teacher who didn't make me feel stupid because I didn't get it. You see, I'm dyslexic and didn't learn to read until I was 20, and it's a miracle that I was ever able to become a writer."

"Would you like some water?" asked the little short nun with the curly grey hair. "Yes," I said. "Please."

She quickly got up and went to the two large tables where the food had been laid out, poured me a glass of water from a large pitcher, and then brought the water and a handful of napkins for me.

"Thank you," I said, taking the water and napkins to dry my eyes. "And you are?" "Mary, Sister Mary, but just call me Mary," she said.

"Thank you, Mary," I said, drinking down the whole glass and then wiping my tears. "Are you the one who wrote me the note and put the rose in the little bag?"

"Yes," she said, getting slightly embarrassed, "but please just go on. We really want to know who this man is who wrote *Rain of Gold.* Most of us girls just knew that it had to be a woman."

I laughed. "Well, in a way it really was a woman," I said, "because it was my mother and my aunts and my godmother whom I interviewed, and *mi papa* had also been raised in the old Indian way as a woman by his old Indian mother for the first seven years of his life, meaning that he learned to do the work around the house and helped in the birthing process of the goats and dogs and cats, and then even of his older cousins and sisters, and such a man," I now added, "doesn't grow up thinking that women are the weaker sex, but instead is in complete awe of women, and this is one of the Eight Indigenous Concepts that will help reverse the course of modern civilization."

I could see that my mention of the Eight Native American Concepts that would take all of us Back To The Future had rattled a lot of cages, but I couldn't stop and explain now, and so I quickly went on.

"But anyway," I said, "getting back to the story of my little nun, my dad had always told me that the most important decision any man can make in his life is choosing the right woman to marry, because the woman a man married would not just be his wife but the first teacher of his children. And so after a couple of weeks of being with my little nun every day after school, I could see that she was by far the kindest, smartest, most wonderful woman I'd ever met, and so naturally I asked her if she would marry me when I grew up. But she told me that she was already married to Jesus.

"'He's dead, you know,' I'd said "'Yes, but I'm married to Our Lord Jesus in Spirit,' she'd said.

"'Oh, then that's okay,' I'd said, 'we can get married in body and have babies.' "And she then smiled this most beautiful smile, and looking back, I can guess that she was now going to explain to me what she meant by being married in Spirit, but she never got to say this to me, because at that very moment the big mother superior came bursting in through the door and she slapped me so hard she knocked me out of my chair, called me the devil, and then started hitting my kind, wonderful, little nun who wouldn't fight back or even try to defend herself, and so this was when I attacked the old nun, biting her leg so hard that she quit hitting my little nun.".

I stopped. My heart was pounding. And I could see that I'd startled half of the nuns, and others were in tears, but the priests, a few of them looked like they now wanted to hit me, too.

"But now let's not stop here," I said, heart still pounding, "because I'd like to bring that incident that happened 40-some years ago to the present and ask how many of you had experiences with a little kid like this? And you don't have to raise your hands. No, what I really want for you to do is ... is to just go within yourself, to your own Kingdom of God, and see if you ever behaved like this mother superior or the little nun, because that wasn't the end of that situation.

"Oh, no, after that, the young priest, who was attached to the school and the old mother superior, thought it was their duty to keep beating me on a weekly schedule and tell me that I'd been born with Original Sin and so they were punishing me for my own good, so I wouldn't go to hell and burn for eternity."

I wiped the tears out of my eyes. "But now looking back, what I think was really going on was that both, that young priest and the old mother superior, were in love with my beautiful young nun and they were jealous that they'd never proposed marriage to her."

I glanced around. "And I'm not joking," I added. "Recently, I've had the good fortune to become friends with some ex-nuns and ex-sisters of different religious organizations, and they've told me that part of the reason they left their organizations was because of the sexual advances that had been made on them by their superiors, both male and female."

I stopped, taking in a deep breath. "And I'm not blaming or finger pointing. I'm just saying that there are no accidents in life, and that we are a very emotional and sexually driven planet, and so we need to understand this and admit it, so that then everyday can, indeed, become *otro milagro de Dios,* instead of a living hell, because of all of our hypocrisy, and hidden agendas and lies.

"And so yes, I'm glad that I came to see you guys, because the buck needs to stop here, right now, so together we can do some serious healing, and … and not just of the body and mind, but also of our Hearts and Souls." I breathed and then added, "And so thank you, thank all of you here very much for having invited me to come to see you, for you and I now have a great—" Two priests had gotten to their feet. "No, please, don't leave!" I said. "This is good! This is wonderful!"

"Yes, he's right, you know," said a tall elegant nun who was sitting beside little Sister Mary. "Mother Teresa always says, "I know that God will not give me anything I can't handle, but I only wish that He didn't have so much trust in me."

Many of the nuns nodded in agreement, but I could see that quite a few of the priests looked like they were ready to bolt, and not just these two who'd stood up. I closed my eyes, asked for guidance, then decided to take the bull by the horns.

"Look," I said to the two priests, "leave if you must, but also realize that this will only cause people to think the worst of you." I opened my eyes. "And so I suggest that you two stay and we all see this through together. Because, like my mother so well said to me before I left, '*Mijito*, all my life I've found that miracles often come to us when we least expected it, and when we're doing exactly what it is that we've been avoiding and not wanting to do.' And then my mother told me to open up my heart and pray and realize that there are no accidents, only situations that can cause us to Spiritually grow beyond our wildest dreams. So please, stay and ... and let us dream together."

"Yes," spoke the tall, elegant-looking nun again, "and this was exactly what Teresa was talking about and ... and what is now causing me to have to consider if I ever behaved like that mother superior when I was in that position."

"Thank you," I said to this ex-mother superior, "this is truly wonderful, and so now what I'm proposing is that we all fasten our seatbelts because ... because we're now going into the Kingdom of God that's within each of us, and hence OUT, OUT, OUT TO THE FURTHEST STARS, and into a reality beyond our five-sensory perception and into OUR NATURAL MULTI-SENSORY PERCEPTION OF 13 SENSES, AND INFINITE POSSIBILITIES!

"And this is no joke! But the very foundation of *Rain of Gold,* which means a rain of Miracles coming down to us from God on a daily basis! You see, most people miss the point and simply read *Rain* as a history book about two families and the Mexican Revolution, and then coming to the United States, but this isn't what *Rain of Gold* is really all about. It's about—"

"Faith in God!" said Sister Mary. "And about learning to see nature in a way that I'd never read about in any other book, and then your mother Lupe, a seven-year-old child, waking up every day to the first three miracles of the day."

"It's about a family, who in their innocence, still lives in the Garden of Eden, saying that every woman needs her own crying tree, and then butterflies coming into their box canyon in a dancing cloud of dazzling golden color and land among all the beautiful wild orchids and other gorgeous flowers!" said another nun.

"It's about the love of a seven-year-old girl for her knight in shining armor, and how she has to make tough decisions that would intimidate even grown women."

"It's about forgiveness and gratitude and going on, no matter what." "It's about seeing every day as another Miracle given to us by God."

"It's about life and a kind loving God, and never getting bitter, even after witnessing your children being raped and killed before your very eyes."

"Yes," said Sister Mary, turning to the nun who'd spoken last, "but it doesn't stop there. Even after *Doña Margarita,* my favorite character, looses 11 of her 14 children, she still goes to her outhouse, smokes her little *cigarillo,* drinks her coffee laced with *whiskito,* and she says her rosary. Oh, to have such relaxed, natural Faith no matter what, this is what *Rain of Gold* is really all about!"

I pulled up a chair and sat down and my eyes filled with tears of joy. These nuns had really read *Rain of Gold* and they'd really, really gotten it, but the priests, as a group, still didn't join them.

"Oh, my God, thank you, thank you, thank you!" I said, getting up, after half of the nuns had spoken. "And I almost didn't come. Oh, what a Doubting Thomas I am! But truly, I can now see that we're going to have a fine time, because I can now see that a lot of you here are ready to receive beyond your wildest dreams! You see, myself, I've been receiving beyond my wildest dreams ever since I took an oath before God up in the wilds of Wyoming to become not just a writer, but a writer as great as Homer and/or greater with the help of Our Lord God."

"How old were you?" asked a priest.

"Oh, nineteen, or maybe a week into being 20. I'd just gotten back from México where I'd found my roots just as Alex Haley had found his in Africa."

"You were only 19 when you took that oath?" asked this same priest.

"Well, why not? Didn't most of you here take a similar oath at 18, 19, or 20 to dedicate your lives to the service of God? So that's what I did, too. But I can tell you that it wasn't until my dad passed over and I was in my late 40s that my Spiritual Education EXPLODED INTO MIRACLES! And I then came to the full realization that I'd been receiving from the University of the Divine ever since I'd taken my oath. And you guys have also been receiving from this same Divine University whether you realize it or not.

"And this evening after dinner," I continued, "I'll be able to guide you on how to receive in your sleep, just as my dad explained to me on the night before he passed over. And then tomorrow morning I'll ask you about your dreams, and you'll see how, as a group, as a Collective Consciousness of Dreaming, you people will start leading, and I'll be the one who'll start following in front!"

"Following in front?" asked a priest.

"Yes, that's what the big male goose does when he's at the head of a V- formation of geese, cutting the wind so that all the rest of the geese can then use 30% less energy to keep up. But no more about this right now. Right now I need for all of you to fasten your seatbelts, because ... because we first need to gain the understanding of the Eight Western Civilization Concepts that are holding us back from worldwide Harmony and Peace and Abundance for All, and once we grasp these eight concepts, we will then be able to slipslide back into the Indigenous Concepts that will free us, then BOOM! We explode into Our Natural All-Knowing Cellular Memory, and each of you will then start remembering that we come from the Stars, Our True Home, and you'll also Know deep inside of yourself all about Our Six Sister Planets that Our Mother Earth belongs to.

"You see, all of you already Know all this deep inside your Collective Cellular Memory, and this is why Jesus so well said that what He did, we, Collectively, would do more, and in doing more, we will automatically Harmonize into World Wide Peace and Abundance for All, because this is a natural part of our DNA, and all of our Six Sister Planets have already realized this eons of timeless time ago!"

The same two priests leaped to their feet.

"Oh, please," I said, closing my eyes, "just sit your asses back down! Didn't Jesus say that we all have the Kingdom of God within us? Well, then, the Kingdom of God must include everything there is, and so I'm not really saying anything new! Come on, guys, just sit back down, and I promise you that all this will start making sense in just a little bit.

"You see," I said, opening my eyes, "*Rain of Gold* is just the first book of a trilogy, so what you people have read is just the tip of the iceberg. Remember, Hemingway said that the dignity of the movement of an iceberg is that 7/8 is under water, and so we're just getting started, guys."

Hearing this, both old priests sat back down.

"Thank you," I said, "thank you very much. You see, I didn't come here with loaded guns. I really did as my mother told me to do and I asked for guidance, and when I went to bed that night I understood that yes, I was supposed to come out here and see you, and then last night, right here, in my room upstairs, *mi papa*, who'd passed over 10 years ago, came to me in my sleep and he assured me that my mother was right, and that it was pre-ordained that all of us come together. So come on, let's just go for it! Okay?" The two priests nodded. "Good. Thank you. And so now I'm going to first start with a little story, and then I'm going to ask you all to join me in a Native American prayer that will set up what this whole talk will really be all about. Okay, ready?"

Once again, all the nuns nodded, but quit a few of the priests still looked pretty guarded.

"Okay, not long ago I read an article about two young *Latino* astronomers," I said, "and the article explained how these two young guys had come to the conclusion that all the telescopes around the world had grey-green lenses, and that grey-green wasn't part of the natural colors of a rainbow. So these two guys then speculated that if the rainbow color of rose was put on the huge telescope in Baja, California, where the sky is still relatively clean and there are no city lights for 100s of miles, then these new stars that had recently been found would turn out not to be stars, but entire new galaxies and galaxies, because of the higher frequency of their natural rose-colored lens.

"Well, these two young Chicano astronomers were finally able to get the funding to do it, and they found out that these new stars were, indeed, new galaxies and new galaxies, and then when they turned their rose-colored lenses to other well-established parts of the heavens, they discovered other new galaxies, too, and our comprehension of the heavens quadrupled exponentially, and they almost hadn't been allowed to do their work by the old well-established astronomers. Pretty good, eh? And so this is what I'm now proposing that we do. That we put on rose-colored glasses like in that old Frank Sinatra song, and that you please join me in this Native American prayer that I learned from my good friend Lydia Whirlwind Soldier of the Lakota Nation.

"Eh, would you please do me the honor and join me? You see, this is also what my two Indigenous *mamagrandes* always did. They'd wouldn't look at the world through the low frequency of the grey-green glasses of Western Civilization, but instead, they'd keep their vibrant rose-colored glasses on, and they'd mix their Indian Spirituality with their Catholic Christianity, and, in doing this, they'd come up with a wonderful new way of giving Daily Thanks to Our Holy Creator. All right, now everyone please stand up!" All the nuns immediately stood up. The priests were a little slower to follow, but they all finally got to their feet, too.

"Okay, good," I said. "Thank you. And now, put your left hand, palm open, and facing up, and put your right hand, palm open, and facing down. Good. Good. Perfect."

All the nuns were participating, but even though all of the priests had stood up, only about half of them were doing what I asked. I closed my eyes. I was not going to let this bother me. I sent them all Love*Amor,* and then when I opened my eyes, a few more of the priests began participating. And I also noticed that the young, very handsome priest, who was sitting next to Father James, looked totally open and big happy.

"Okay, now, please, everyone close your eyes," I said, "and breathe in deeply, activating your Kingdom of God that Jesus so wisely told us about. Good. Good. And now imagine yourself to be a Hollow Bone. A Buffalo Bone. And with your left hand facing up and open, you are receiving, receiving, receiving good-feeling harmonious energy from our whole entire Universe! Just like Albert Einstein did when he received his great theory!" I said with a loud clear voice and with my eyes still closed. "And with your right hand open and facing down you are flooding the Mother Earth with all this good, wonderful, healthy, Pure Love Energy you are receiving even from the ... the FURTHEST REACHES OF THE UNIVERSE!

"Breathe, breathe, and realize that the faster you give, the faster you receive, so you keep giving and giving and giving as you keep receiving and receiving and ... and receiving, and you keep *nada, nada,* nothing for yourself, because you are a Hollow Bone, a Buffalo Bone, and you are so huge, so great that your head and hands and feet stretch out to the ends of Creation; receiving, receiving, receiving, and Our Sacred Mother Earth is no larger than a grain of sand on the Seashore of Creation, and we, Human Beings, are Holy Instruments of receiving and giving.

"And understand that old Albert knew this to his bones! That we are all Hollow Bones! Buffalo Bones once we've activated the Kingdom of God that's within each of us! And then at this point we, all of us, become the Almighty's Holy instruments of spreading His/Her Love*Amor* throughout the Universe! Because this is who we, Human Beings, really are, Holy Sacred Instruments of receiving and giving and this is why, when I was eight years old, I was able to receive the vision of seeing my brother Joseph, three days after he'd passed over, walking on the ocean just out beyond the breakers alongside Jesus."

"You saw Jesus?"

I opened my eyes. "Yes, I saw Jesus," I said.

"In full three-dimensional form?"

"Well, yes, of course, but please, just let me go on, because, you see, the time has come in our Godelution for all of us to start walking alongside Jesus right now, right here on Mother Earth."

"Godelution?" mumbled another priest, opening his eyes, too.

"Yes," I said, "Godelution is also one of the Eight Indigenous Concepts that we need in order for us to slipslide and/or dissolve ourselves back into the Holy Garden. Evolution and God do not necessary have to oppose each other."

"Makes perfect sense!" shouted a nun, who was keeping her eyes closed. "Not to me," said a priest, opening his eyes.

And I could now see that almost everyone had their eyes open.

"Okay," I said to the priest, "I can understand why you'd say that, but now tell me, have you ever walked into a room and you instantly knew something was wrong? Come on, how many of you have had this experience?"

Almost everyone raised their hands, especially the nuns who still had their eyes closed.

"Good. Excellent. And you didn't think this," I said, "you knew this, because thinking is done with manmade words which are very recent in our development as Human Beings, and on the other hand, feelings are ancient. Maybe 100s of 1000s of years old, if not millions of years, and we feel not just done with our hands, but with our whole body 26 arm-lengths in all directions.

"And old cops immediately know what I'm talking about, because when they come to a potentially violent situation, they automatically quit their thinking and start trusting their gut-feelings, their instinct, which is the voice of our genius which processes information 10,000 times faster than thinking."

I stopped and glanced around. Only a few still had their eyes closed. "And so what I'm saying," I continued, "is that we all now need to quit our thinking, so we can get out of our Head Computer and move into our Heart Computer, and only then can we access our Soul Computer, and enter into the Kingdom of God that's within each of us.

"Truly understand that our five senses we got from the Greeks, from Aristotle, I believe, is one of the Eight Western Concepts that is holding us back, and our Full Natural 13 Multi-Sensory Perception, that came to me from my *mamagrande* from *Oaxaca, México,* will free us, because we do, in fact, have three computers for processing information. The Head Computer with four senses, the Heart Computer with three senses, and the Soul Computer with six senses, and 'thinking' is to the Head Center as 'intuition' is to the Heart Center and 'psychic powers' are to the Soul Center. This is why I was able to tell Obama 20-some years ago in South Chicago that he was going to be President of the United States for two terms and his greatest work would happen six months after he left the oval office, and why I also knew — like Bishop Malachy of Ireland knew back in the 12th Century — that our next Pope, number 112, will be our last Pope, because the Vatican will be moving to Ireland for 100 years, where we will have Our First Lady Pope, then the Vatican will move to *Oaxaca, México* for 100 years, and will keep moving every 100 years for the next 50,000 years so it can keep growing, expanding, and changing just like all the rest of Creation."

Hands were going up all over the place. I closed my eyes. "Please, no, no, questions yet. Right now, please just breathe. Breathe and understand that the longest journey any of us will ever make are those 18 inches from our head to our Heart Center and then to our Soul Center."

I stopped and breathed. "Good, good," I said, laughing. "I can now see that most of you are participating with me and breathing deeply, or you are shaking your heads and your eyes are wide open with very mixed feelings. Excellent! And so now I'd like you to know that that Native American prayer we just did is one key for moving us those eighteen inches. Eh, it felt pretty good deep inside to see yourselves as Hollow Bones! Buffalo Bones! As God's Sacred Instruments for spreading Love*Amor* throughout the Universe!"

A lot of people nodded, saying yes.

"Good. I'm glad to hear this, because I'll tell you, the first time I heard this prayer, it touched me to the depths of my being. My God, for us to be the Sacred Instruments of spreading Love*Amor* for God was so beautiful! So fantastic! And made so much sense! Then we, Human Beings, really can walk on water alongside Jesus because we're part of God's Creating Light. And this, in a nutshell, is what Albert Einstein did to receive his theory and what I'll be talking about for the next two days. Okay, now the rest of you please open your eyes," I said. "And now please turn and look at each other. Do you now see yourselves differently?" I asked. "Do you see a Light?"

Several nuns nodded and said that they did.

"Good," I said, "so will one of you tell us about this Light you see?"

Mary, the curly grey-haired little nun, spoke first. "When I first opened my eyes I thought I saw a Light surrounding Sister Margret, but now I'm not quite sure."

"Exactly," I said, "when I first began to see a bright and yet soft Golden Light around people, I thought it was just my imagination. But then I also began to see a crescent shaped little Moon just off to my right when I got up to write and I'd go to the bathroom to wash my face. Then it soon began happening to me so regularly that I knew it was really real and not just my imagination.

"So what I'm saying is that this Light that some of you saw, especially you people who kept your eyes closed the whole time so you were able to keep your focus, will now start happening to you more and more regularly, and then BOOM! You, too, will then one day see your own Crescent Moon, and soon that Moon will soon be so bright and steady that you won't have to turn on the bathroom light when you get up in the middle of the night to go to the bathroom. And...and most important, you'll be feeling, oh, so happy! BIG BIG HAPPY!"

"That's true," said Mary. "When I saw this Holy Light surrounding Margret, it was like I was receiving all this understanding, all these feelings that we're all Holy, and that I still have a lot of life to live," she said, with tears of joy coming to her eyes. "Like I now understand that my life of service is far from over, and this makes me so happy!"

"BIG, BIG HAPPY, eh?" I shouted.

"Yes! BIG BIG HAPPY!"

I laughed. She laughed.

"And all of you who were able to keep your eyes closed the whole time, are you now beginning to see that there's a whole world out here, within us, that's Alive with the Living Breath of God?"

"Is this why you continually close your eyes," asked a nun who had not spoken yet, "and take in such deep breaths?"

"Yes, exactly," I said. "And I'd like all of you to notice that when Mary spoke she never used the word 'thinking' in reference to the Light she saw. She used the words 'understanding' and then 'feelings', and this is, because thinking, which processes information through manmade words, is so superficial and limiting that we can never come to Know God with thinking. Albert Einstein wasn't thinking when he came up with his theory. No, he was flashing with Light of Divine Understanding, and this is called receiving through your Guardian Angel and/or Genuising."

"Yes," said a nun in the second row, "it was a wonderful experience for you to have us close our eyes, because with my eyes closed I wasn't distracted even with what was being said, and I actually got to feeling so strongly connected to God that, of course, I just wanted to keep giving and giving forever!"

"Exactly," I said. "You see, greed is not part of human nature. What is part of human nature is birthing God."

"Birthing God!?!" said several priests and one nun.

"Yes, this is another Indigenous Concept that we all used to understand when we remembered our Original Instruction. Why do you think that religions are so strong all over the world? We're all trying to birth God, to give Life to God from deep inside of us. Truly, greed only happens when we lose contact with God that's here within us. You all read how my grandmother *Doña Margarita* gave away all the money that the rich man gave her in *Arandas, Jalisco* when she was on her way to save her son, Jose, the Great, from execution."

"That's not in *Rain of Gold,*" said a couple of nuns.

"Oh, that's right," I said, laughing. "That didn't get into *Rain.* This is in *Wild Steps of Heaven.* You see, originally *Rain* was 1,500 pages, so I ended up breaking it down into three books. Anyway, my dad explained to me that when people think money will solve all of their *problemas,* then it is very difficult if not impossible for them to see or ever receive any Miracles from the Almighty.

"Truly, Collectively, understand that we all need to once more start becoming Hollow Bones, Buffalo Bones, Instruments of receiving God's Holy Light, just as Albert Einstein did when he saw himself riding on that beam of light and he came up with his Theory of Relativity. You see, this is exactly who we, Human Beings, really are once we activate Our Kingdom of God that's within each of us; we become … Beams of the Almighty's Holy Light, giving and giving and giving in ABUNDANCE!

"Remember, Supreme Being is one of the original terms we used for God, and we are Human Beings, and so old Einstein was right when he saw himself riding on a beam of light. No, actually saw himself become a beam of Holy Golden Light, and this is who we all really, really are.

"And I, myself, I could never really grasp this until I first learned to see myself as a Hollow Bone, a Buffalo Bone, a Holy Instrument of receiving and giving and keeping nothing. Then the words Supreme Being and Human Being made sense to me, and I could also then see that when Einstein ShapeShifted and became a Beam of Light, he was then of Total Service for the Greater Glory of God, and this kind of ShapeShifting is another one of the Eight Natural Indigenous Concepts that we need to activate in order for us to slipslide back into our Natural Flow of Godelution."

Three hands shot up. "Yes?" I said.

"Isn't ShapeShifting a term used by Native Americans?"

"Yes, and it can also be called SongShifting. You see, when God created the Universe, He/She created One Song, One United Verse, and so it is really all about Energy Frequencies, meaning that each of us comes to Mother Earth with our very own Song, our own unique Vibrational Frequency. Okay, no more, please. I need a little break, "I said, "and then when we come back we can ... well, understand why it is time in our Godelution for all of us to stop worshipping Jesus and start doing Jesus, because remember Jesus told us that what He did, we would do more?"

"JUST WAIT!" shouted a tall thin priest who was in the back row. "Are you now insinuating you've walked on water?"

"What? Why do you ask this?" I said. I had no idea where he was coming from. "You just said 'do' Jesus, and Jesus walked on water, and so for us to do Jesus, then we, too, would need to walk on water."

I gripped my forehead. I could feel his frustration from clear across the room and I almost said, "What are you so afraid of?" But I didn't and I closed my eyes, asked for guidance, and I immediately knew deep within me that this guy had been a very abusive priest, and only now, that he was old and fearing death, was he beginning to be haunted by what he'd done. I opened my eyes and said, "Father, it's not too late for you to ask God for forgiveness."

Rage exploded across his face. "How dare you speak to me like this!"

I re-closed my eyes. "Please, Father, understand that it's going to be okay. Truly, God is all about Love and nothing but Love*Amor*. It's our own fears that caused us to come up with all this business of an angry God who's full of wrath, and ... and we'll get into all this after our little break. Okay, take ten," I said, and quickly walked out of the room. I needed to get to my room as quickly as I could.

FOUR

Taking two and three stairs at a time, I ran up to the second story and rushed down the hallway to my room. Going inside and closing the door, I rushed into the bathroom, closed that door, and I took the biggest dump I'd ever taken in my life, and it smelled awful! I had to open the window. My God, what was it that was coming out of me? I guess all these years of holding resentment and anger had fermented into a terrible shit inside of me. I went to the sink and washed my hands and my face with cold water. I guess my mother had been right. It really was affecting me deep inside to have come to see these old nuns and priests. I turned off the water and turned to get a towel and this is when I saw that my dad was standing behind me.

"Hello," I said, reaching around him for a towel.

"*Buenos dias,*" he said with a big smile.

"*Papa,*" I said, drying my hands and face, "I need help. I can't do this alone." "You're not alone," said another voice.

I lowered the towel from my face and I saw that my brother Joseph was standing alongside our dad.

"Joseph?" I said. "Oh, wow!"

I hadn't seen my brother in full form since I'd been eight years old and he'd come walking across the water just beyond the breakers with Jesus at his side a few days after he'd passed over.

"We're all here with you," he said. "You have nothing to worry about."

"Really?" I said.

"Yes, just lie down for a few minutes so we can transmit to you," added my brother.

"Transmit? You mean like a radio receives transmissions from their different stations?"

"Yes, through Our Lord we will feed you Heart to Heart and Soul to Soul."

I did as told. I went out of the bathroom, into the bedroom, and fell across my bed and instantly I was out like a light. And when I awoke I felt totally refreshed and ready to go, and looking at the clock by the bed, I could see that I'd only lain down for about eight minutes. It was totally amazing. In just eight minutes it felt as if I'd gained as much rest as a whole night's sleep. But then I remembered that our 8th Sense was Music and Music activated our Soul Computer, and once we moved into this computer, then our 9th Sense, Time, and our 10th Sense, Space, were both relative, and/or disappeared.

I got up. My dad and brother Joseph were both gone, but I knew that they hadn't left me. No, I could still feel them totally here with me. Oh, I was now ready! No more doubt! No more confusion! Now all was smooth sailing inside of me once again. I went whistling down the hallway stairs and I now realized that as a Hollow Bone, a Buffalo Bone, I was being sent Infinite amounts of Love*Amor,* and so of course, I was then supposed to send Infinite Love*Amor* to this priest who'd spoken up.

I went dancing down the hall. My God, I'd never felt better in all my life. Seeing me come into the room, they quickly began taking their seats.

"Good," I said, "I can see that you all came back. Thank you very much. And I want to apologize for my behavior. I had no right to suggest that one of you needed to ask for forgiveness. What I should have done was addressed the question that I'd been asked and that was . . . was I insinuating that I've walked on water. And, well, now the truth is that I didn't know how to answer the question, because—" I blushed. "I had to take a dump, and as it was, I barely made it to my room in time."

People laughed.

"And I'll tell you," I continued, "it turned out being one of the biggest and most awful smelling dumps I've ever taken, and I think it had a lot to do with the fact that I've been holding on to so much crap inside of me for all these years that it had fermented," I added, laughing. "Did anyone else ever have a similar experience?"

Two nuns burst out laughing and nodded their heads, and then the tall, thin priest who'd spoken up, laughed, too.

"I had a big one, too," he said, "and I'm sure that if I hadn't had a big one, I wouldn't have returned."

"Well, I'm very glad that you did," I said, "so we can now address that question of yours. You see, after my dump, my dad and my brother Joseph came to me."

"In spirit?" asked the priest.

"No, yes, I mean, yes, in Spirit, because they've both passed over but they also came to me in full three-dimensional form, and they told me to address your question with a specific question." I breathed. "Tell me, where would we be today if . . . if Peter had not looked down and he had walked side by side with Jesus on water? Eh, where would we all be today?"

I glanced around. My God, the question had really worked. You could hear a pin drop.

"Well, one thing would be for sure," said a nun in the back row who had not spoken, "if Peter hadn't looked down and he'd walked on water alongside Our Lord Jesus, then we wouldn't be as fearful today, because we'd know that if Peter could do this, then maybe we can do it, too."

"We'd all feel closer to Our Lord Jesus," another nun said with tears of joy streaming down her face.

"Everything would be different for us, because we would have been raised to think that walking on water and other such miracles were a normal part of life," said Margret, the tall, elegant nun.

I smiled and they continued and I could now see why I'd been told to address this question with this specific question. A Miracle was taking place before my very eyes. These nuns were now stepping forward and taking the lead.

"My parents would have felt safe to just love me, and not be so critical," said another nun.

So I continued listening and it was beautiful, then I finally said, "Amen! And I now would like you to know that this was how I was raised by my Yaqui Indian *mamagrande,* and so yes, straight out, I can now tell you that no, I haven't walked on water, but I've done much more. You see, back at one time when we were All, All, All Indigenous People the world over, we knew that ordinary people walked on water when they reached our most perfect human age of 78, so water walking wasn't that big a deal between 78 and 104, which is our normal age for passing."

"What in the world are you now talking about?" asked another priest. "I was just beginning to follow you, and now you throw a whole new wrench into this mess!"

"Here, let me explain," I said, "you see within the Multi-Sensory World of 13 Senses our natural aging process also happens in stages of 13 years. And our first 13 is, of course, puberty, give or take a couple of years. Our second is 26 which is our full male and/or female powers. Our next is at 39, and this is when women stop caring what men think or do and they start coming into their own male powers, and in our society at 39 men start looking at young girls because they start feeling the lessening of their male powers and so they feel the need to prove themselves.

"And then 52 is the big one for both sexes because women stop their periods, give or take two years, and they go through men-o-pause, meaning that they pause before they come into their full male powers. Women actually get a little hair on their upper lip and a few around their nipples, and they become Women of Substance. And at this age you met my two grandmothers and you witnessed them being tough and strong. And men at this point, go through women-o-pause and get unsure and kinder and/or mean. Then at 65, both women and men start to balance out their male and female powers, and then at 78 BINGO! People start living with one foot in This World and the other foot in the Other World, and like I earlier said, to the degree that they accept their Spirituality, to that degree there is no aging between 78 to 104."

"How do you know all this?" asked a priest.

I looked at him and I could see that his question was sincere. "Because," I said to him, "I was educated in our Original Instructions by my Yaqui Indian *mamagrande* before I started school and my parents followed up that education, because they, too, had been home educated by their mothers and grandmothers, and then on the night my dad passed, he told me that he'd be coming back to educate from the University of the Divine once he checked in with his mother, the rest of our *Familia*, and the Grand Masters."

"And we, too, can receive this Divine Education?" asked the same priest. "Absolutely," I said. "Look about three years back, I was the keynote speaker in Seattle, and after I'd spoken I went to one of the workshops and this big burly guy with a huge grey beard sprinkled with a lot of red was leading the workshop. His audience was mostly teachers and administrators, and he asked them if they'd ever had the experience of driving in a mall parking lot and had a group of young teenage boys about 14 and 15 walking real slow in front of them. Most of the people raised their hands.

"He laughed and gave a slow strutting gait to demonstrate his point, then said, 'And if you're dumb enough to honk at them, what do they do? They don't get out of your way. Oh, no, they turn and look at you as if you're the one with a problem, and now they walk even slower. So who's had this experience?' With laughter, almost everyone raised their hands. 'And now I want you to know that those boys were doing exactly what they are supposed to be doing,' he said, 'because Socialization is 100s of 1000s of years old, if not millions of years, and Civilization is only 20 to 40,000 years old at best, and we are trying to get boys to conform to Civilization instead of Socialization.'

"Then he explained to us that when young male bear cubs reach this age of about 200 pounds and they start behaving this way, their mothers take them to a spot where they know the bear cub can make it on his own and they leave them and never return. 'At first the male cub gets angry,' he said to us, 'but then as night falls he gets scared, and by daybreak he's so hungry that he starts to fend for himself. And it used to be that when boys got to be 14 and 15 year old, we'd push them out of the nest like the Falcons do, but now in modern times we can't just throw them out of our homes, because we educate our kids for school and college, and not for life, and so they're tough where they should be kind, and wild when they should be cautious. And we parents do this because we have lost our Original Instructions, and don't have a clue how to live a sustainable life or how to pass on information to our children.'

"This was the first time I'd ever heard the term Original Instructions and that there used to be a way to live in harmony with nature instead of conquering the wild and raping our planet. And then he told us that little female bears were kept for about a year longer, so the mother could give her the advanced knowledge of how to be a mother bear, and he told us that he'd learned all this from the Native Americans of the Northwestern United States. I could have listened to that big burly guy all day long. He was wonderful! And he was validating how I'd been raised, telling us things just like my *mamagrande* used to tell me, and he said to us that the ducks and geese knew when to migrate, and salmon knew when to go down river and out to sea and then with their last dying breath they knew how to fight back upstream and spawn.

"And so now after sharing all this background, I can answer your question of how come I know all this. Simply, I came to know all of this because I was raised with the understanding that every day is *otro milagro de Dios,* and so of course, Peter could have walked on water, because when people reached this most perfect age of 78, with one foot on This Side of Living and another on the Other Side of Living, it was then normal to walk on water and perform Daily Miracles.

"And all of you here in this room are at this age and/or approaching this perfect age of 78, and so it's now time for all of you to go for it! And not into retirement, but to go into Inspirement! Because... because you are OUR SACRED ELDERS! Look, Miracles are our norm! My whole family and I have done more than just walk on water! We have walked on fire that was measured at 1,200 Fahrenheit, and we've had L.A. rush hour traffic part for us like the Red Sea so we could travel at 60, 70, 90 miles an hour while all the rest of the traffic crept along at 5 and 10 miles an hour, and personally I've walked off a 30 foot rock cliff into thin air, and ... and God assisted my every step by providing a rock staircase that allowed me to get down from the cliff.

"Remember in *Rain* when my mother Lupe turned into a fern so those renegade soldiers wouldn't rape her and kill her? And do you remember when my dad turned into stone along with the two Yaqui Indians so the prison guards and their pack of dogs didn't tear them to pieces. And both of these Miracles are forms of ShapeShifting, SongShifting, and/or Ghosting, and my parents were able to do them, because my parents had been taught in the old Indian Way how to Breathe in God with their every Breath, and then with the Sacred Holy Breath of God you can do—"

"JUST WAIT!" shouted a priest. "Are you then saying that you didn't write all of these things as metaphors? And your mother Lupe actually turned into a fern?"

"Yes," I said, taking in a deep breath. "This is exactly what I'm saying, and why I got 265 rejections before I got published and ... and why my New York publisher wanted to bring out *Rain* as fiction, and why my mother—God bless her soul—was willing to mortgage her home, her last possession in the world, so we could buy the rights back from Putnam." Tears came to my eyes. "My mom was in her 80s!" I yelled.

"My dad had passed! And still she had the guts, the ovaries, to mortgage her home and ... and ... oh, my God!" I said, "Can't you see it? All of Life, *la Vida,* is an ONGOING MIRACLE ONCE WE OPEN UP OUR HEART AND SOUL EYES, and begin to see that we live within Seven Dimensions here in our Sacred Holy Mother Earth!"

I stopped, wiping the tears out of my eye. "And you guys just glimpsed that," I added, "when you saw how different our world would be if Peter had walked on water. So let's not lose that vision that we all just had together, because ... because what I'm saying is that we all need to get beyond Peter and take Jesus off all the crosses in the world and stop worshipping Him and start being like Him. This was His message. Not that negative story of Him needing to save us from our sins, but instead a positive story of Him coming to Mother Earth to INSPIRE US TO GREATNESS!

"Just imagine what a world we would have if all Christians were into forgiveness, as Our Lord Jesus did on the cross, instead of being so judgmental and into finger pointing, and thinking that their way was the only way. And this is exactly why He came to me when I was eight, so I could learn that when one of our loves passes over, we don't lose them," I said with more tears coming to my eyes, "but instead we gain an even closer relationship with Jesus, and this is also why He came to me in Spain and why He even came to me last night, here at your place, because Jesus has ALWAYS BEEN ALL ABOUT POSITIVE LOVING *AMOR* AND INCLUSIVE ENERGY!

"You see, it's simply out of date for us to be living in fear of God, and it's out of date to—here, let me tell you a story that will show you that people have really, really, really been walking on water all over the world for eons of timeless time. Okay, ready?" I said, walking away from the podium and getting an empty chair out of the front row and turning it around so I could face them.

"Oh, yeah, this feels so much closer and so much more better," I said, laughing, then I closed my eyes. "In the hallway to my writing room, I have an old black and white picture of Einstein riding a bicycle. He's my hero, because he's happy. Big Big Happy! And this is where we are all now going! Ready? Good. Good. And now just close your eyes, so you don't get distracted and you can slipslide into our Collective Happy Consciousness of the Kingdom of God."

People closed their eyes and I could feel a hush come over the room. And I could also feel that all of the nuns were with me, but the priests, for the most part, were either ready to bolt and/or were shitting square bricks. And sure I understood that I'd take them out of their comfort zone, but I wasn't going to slow down. No, I had to keep going if we were ever going to get anywhere.

"All right," I now said, opening my eyes and looking at the tall, old priest, "and to now address your question about walking on water, or parting the Red Sea, or any of those other old Miracles of the Bible, let me share with you this story about my Great Great Great Great Great Aunt, Mother Of No Specific Child, who, like so many of our Sacred Elders, became a Miracle Maker and a Water Walker at the Blessed Age of 78.

"And so my dad told me that one afternoon our aunt was walking on water from peninsula to peninsula doing her Sacred Holy Healing Work down in the lower part of México when some young Spanish soldiers saw her walking across the water. Instantly they dropped to their knees and started praying, thinking she was of Jesus Christ, but when the old priest found out about this, he screamed blasphemy, and he had her arrested and raped and burned at the stake, so he could prove to these young soldiers that she was of the devil and not of Jesus Christ.

"But it backfired on the old priest." I said, getting out of my chair, "for a young priest named Jose-Maria saw her dignity and purity of love even as she burned, and so he knew that she was, indeed, of Our Lord Jesus Christ. Jose-Maria ripped off his collar and a bunch of the young soldiers joined him and together they united with the local Indians and they revolted against the Church and Spain with SUCH CONVICTION that they almost turned the tide of the European invasion!

"And this, all this, you will, of course, never find in any history book, but this is what my dad told me that his mother *Doña Margarita* told him, and her father *Don Pio* told her, and *Don Pio's* mother told him, and now the big one, that I'd like all of you to know, is that from the Other Side, my dad also told me that our Great Great Great Great Great Aunt, Mother Of No Specific Child, was 165 years old when she was arrested, tortured, and then burned at the stake, and so she was Totally of Jesus!" I added, with tears streaming down my face.

"And you say your dad told you all of this from the Other Side?" asked a nun.

I nodded. "Yes, I don't think he even mentioned her when he was on This Side of Living," I said.

"Why do you think he never did?" asked the same nun.

I laughed. "Look, I had enough trouble believing in the big snake my dad told me about and the dancing clouds of butterflies that my mother spoke to me about, so I'm sure my dad knew that only after he passed over and came to me in my sleep, educating me from the University of the Divine, would I be able to hear him and accept what he told me. And this is what we'll do today after dinner. I'll give you the Tools of Genius that my dad gave me on the night he passed in order for you to receive in your sleep as I've been receiving ever since my dad passed. And all this is being written about in a book called *Beyond Rain of Gold*, but this book will not come out until after *Burro Genius* and *CrazyLoco Love* come out," I added.

"Then you truly believe that your father comes to you in your sleep and it's not just wishful thinking?" asked a priest, with that well practiced little smile of superiority.

And seeing this smile, all the abuses of my childhood came exploding up inside of me and I almost rushed across the room to grab this arrogant old priest by the throat and yank him out of his chair, but I didn't. No, instead I breathed deeply and I closed my eyes, asked for help, and I was immediately told very clear to address his question with a specific question. I opened my eyes.

"Tell me," I said, "do you believe in the Bible?"

"Well, yes, of course, but the Bible is the word of God," he added.

"Okay, I understand that that's what you've been taught to believe, and ... and particularly because of the word 'the' which is only European based, but we'll get into that later. And right now," I said, "what I'd like to know is did you read *Rain of Gold?*"

His face caved in. Oh, yes, I'd been given the right question. "Well, not all of it," he said.

"How much is not all of it?" I asked.

"I read the first part of it, and glanced through the rest," he said.

I closed my eyes. "Look," I said, "I didn't become a writer because I wanted to get rich or famous. Hell, I didn't even like books. I became a writer because I made a deal with God." I opened my eyes. "I was 19 years old and I'd just gotten back from México a few days before, and I'd been happy in México. My stomach didn't hurt. But my dad had explained to me that the United States was now our home, that my older uncles and cousins had paid in blood for this country in World War II and Korea and that my two grand-mothers were buried here.

"So I returned to the U.S. with my dad and I'd only been here a few days and my stomach was hurting once again with all the racism I saw against Mexicans and Blacks. A hate and rage came exploding up inside of me, especially now that I was no longer ashamed of being Mexican, but actually proud of my Indigenous Ancestry!"

I took in a deep breath and blew out fast. "Oh, I was so full of rage that I wanted to kill all of the abusive teachers I've had in public school and also in Catholic school, but then it came to me to pack my rifle and handguns and a few thousand rounds of ammo and get out of town. I got our old ranch truck and took off. I drove east to the rising Father Sun through the back country of Southern California, and then through Las Vegas, Nevada, and St. George, Utah, then north to the southern tip of Idaho, and here I turned east and was going across Wyoming when a herd of antelope ran across the road in front of me. I slammed on my brake, got my Winchester .06 model 70, my .357 Smith and Wesson revolver, and my always-with-me backpack, and took off after the antelope to kill them.

"But then I saw they had yearlings and these little ones looked so innocent. They weren't even afraid of me. In fact, two of them came towards me to see what I was. I guess they'd never seen a human before. And this was when I saw the beautiful snow capped Teton Mountains and I remembered that my *mamagrande* had always told me that it was our job to help *Papito Dios* plant His/ Her ongoing Garden of Heaven on Mother Earth. I began to cry, and then screamed, demanding God to tell me how I could plant any Stardust Seeds with all this rage and hate I had inside of me!

"All this I've written in a book called *CrazyLoco Love* which is the second book of the *Burro Genius* trilogy and this is when God spoke to me, not in words, but in flashes of understanding and I learned that God never chose the Jews. No, it was the Jews who chose God when they took their oral story and put it into written form.

"And in that moment of utter clarity, I understood that there were 1000s and 1000s of Bibles that needed to be written from all over Africa, Asia, and the Americas before we could have peace on earth, and that I, myself, had to write my own people's Holy Book, so we, too, could then become the Chosen People of God like the Jews.

"So, please," I now said to this priest, "no more questions, and especially not from you guys who ... who haven't even read *Rain of Gold* in its entirety, because ... BECAUSE I DIDN'T WRITE IT!" I screamed. "It came through me just as Einstein's theory came through him and Edison's stuff all came through him and ... and ... also understand that I'm not accusing you of being a bad person or anything like that. Hell, I mean, Heaven, I, too, was a Doubting Thomas until my dad passed over in March of 1988, and then he came to me a few months later in New York City in my hotel room, and ever since, he's the one who's been giving me an education straight from Heaven."

I stopped.

I had to sit down. I was shaking, I was so upset. That old priest had no idea how close I'd came to rushing across the room and slapping that little grin off his face.

"And he's right," said Sister Mary. "You wouldn't even be asking these questions if you'd read the book as we asked you to!!" She was pissed!

"I suggest that we listen to Victor. May I call you Victor?" asked Margret. "Of course," I said.

"I suggest that we listen to him as if he's teaching us how to fly a plane," she said, "or as if he's guiding us through this new world of computers."

"Thank you," I said, calming down and wiping the tears out of my eyes. "Thank you very much, and to learn how to fly and/or use a computer there is an entire new language of concepts that we need to learn. Thank you, sister. Your suggestion will be a big help."

"Call me *Margarita*, if you don't mind. *Margarita* like your grandmother."

I smiled. "Of course, *Margarita*," I said to her.

Six hands shot up.

"No, please, no more questions," I said, laughing. "In fact, no more words, no more talking. Let's all just take a little break, so we can digest all this within our own Kingdom of God, then BOOM! We'll come back and go for it ALL THE WAY BACK TO THE FUTURE!"

"It's almost lunch time," announced Father James, standing up, "so why don't we just call it quits for this morning's session."

And as I went out of the room, out of the corner of my eye, I saw that Father James was aglow with a bright and yet soft golden light. Oh, my God, this priest was an Archangel!

FIVE

This time I did not go to my room. I went out the door towards the lake, and the honkers immediately greeted me with their honking. I laughed and said, "hello" to them and continued down the grassy knoll to the lake. Oh, the air smelled so crisp and fresh, and I needed to get away from everyone. I'd never expected this whole thing to go as it had gone. Wow! I'd never thought I'd get into all this heavy stuff, especially not right away. I thought that I'd first start out by telling these old nuns and priests why it was that I'd first fallen in love with the Holy Roman Catholic Church at St. Patrick's in Carlsbad, with the smells and happy sounds of the altar boys pretending to sing back to the old half deaf priest in Latin, but they were actually singing back in Spanish about the best way to cook wild turkey and Mexican green sauce.

And then I figured that after saying this to the old nun and priests and getting them laughing, I'd tell them why I'd quit being a Catholic with a capital 'C,' simply meaning 'universal' as all Catholics are taught, and I was now a catholic with a small 'c' using the full definition of the word which according to the Webster New World Dictionary of American Language was 'universal; all-inclusive; of general interest in value; hence having broad sympathies or understanding; liberal,' and now I felt so much closer to God. And so I was walking along thinking all this and feeling happy and enjoying the sight of all the honkers and deer and the beautiful clear blue water, when that youngish priest came running up to me. He was all out of breath.

"Oh, I'm so glad to catch you alone," he said. "I'm Mark," he added.

"You're a priest, aren't you?" I said, because priests normally didn't give you their first name when they introduced themselves.

"Well, yes, but not for much longer," he said. "You see, I'm leaving the priesthood and getting married."

"Married?" I said.

"Yes, I, too, proposed to a nun," he said.

"Oh," I said, laughing, "then this explains why I've seen you smiling all the time. You're in love."

"Yes, I'm definitely in love," he said. "And I've never been in love like this before."

"And it feels wonderful, eh?"

"Oh, yes, of course, and best of all, I don't feel guilty about being in love and she doesn't either. But, well, it was really very difficult for both of us at first, because of all the pressure that was put on us."

"I can only imagine," I said, putting my hand on his shoulder, "that took a lot of guts. Why do you think they call it 'falling in love', eh? It's scary."

He laughed. "You're right. It has been the scariest thing I've ever done in my life, "he said. "The feelings I was feeling were so powerful and confusing and real!"

"Exactly, because for a person to truly allow himself to fall in love, not only takes a leap of faith as much as walking on water, but then to walk down the aisle to join hands in marriage is a commitment that takes guts way beyond all reasonable comprehension."

"Well, talking about guts," he said, "we read in *People Magazine* about you buying the rights back to *Rain of Gold* from your publisher."

"Yes," I said, "and it all got started with an article in *Publisher's Weekly* where Joe Baro – something wrote about my old mother mortgaging her home so we could buy the rights of *Rain of Gold* back from Putnam, my New York publisher, for $75,000, and how I then got blackballed all over New York."

"And you ended up going with a small press at the University of Houston," he said.

"Exactly," I said, "for 1,500 dollars, and this is when I become a Born Again Texan and reporters came at me from across the country. Everyone was astonished.

But my *familia* and I weren't. My parents' story wasn't fiction," I added. "But now, please, no more about that. Tell me about you and this nun. What's her name?"

"*Josefina*," he said, pronouncing her name with a beautiful *Latino* song-like softness.

"*Josefina*," I repeated, but I couldn't quite say it as romantically.

We continued walking on the grass along the edge of the lake and he told me how Sister Josefina and he had met while working together in Ecuador, and they'd been very good friends for nearly a year, but then at an All Saints Day celebration, which were always such large events throughout Latin America, they'd been so happy and excited together that it had frightened them.

"I'll never forget," he said, "it was a full moon and there were fireworks and kids running all around us and something happened to us, and we just looked at each other in a way that we'd never looked at each other before. So for the next few days we both avoided each other, but then I began to dream of *Josefina* in a way that I'd never dreamed of her previously. And a few years before, I would have gone to confession and asked for forgiveness for the kind of dreams I was having, but not now. Now I knew deep in my heart and soul that these dreams weren't a sin, but instead wonderful and a whole new way of viewing love and life itself, and ... and I then realized I could no longer be a priest. And strangely enough, this was also when I began to understand that Jesus, as a man, must've loved Mary Magdalene. How could He have not? Because my love for *Josefina* felt so natural and good."

He stopped talking and I saw he had tears running down his face, so I took him by his shoulders and turned him around and hugged him. He was trembling and having trouble breathing. My

God, these dreams that he'd had for *Josefina* must've frightened him to no end. He hugged me back, squeezing me with all his might.

"Good," I said, "good. We all need to hug."

"Yes, I can see that now," he said, releasing me, "but I couldn't at first. Oh, all year I'd seen *Josefina* be the kindest, most loving human I'd ever met, just as you spoke about your own little nun. And so finally I, too, got up the nerve to go to her and tell her of my love for her and that I was leaving the priesthood, because I would never again feel ashamed of the feelings that I had for her. She began to cry, saying that she felt the same way about me, and that she, too, would not allow anyone to make her feel ashamed of her feelings, and this was when we took each other in our arms in a whole new way and ... and then we announced our intent of leaving and getting married and we were, well, immediately separated and I was sent here and ... and she was sent to a convent."

"What? You mean you've lost her?" I asked.

"Oh, no," he said. "We were told that we'd have to be six months apart, so we could pray and ask for guidance before we can legally leave the Church and marry. And it's now been 5 months, 16 days, and 12 hours, and 36 minutes," he said, glancing at his wristwatch with the biggest smile I'd ever seen on a human being.

"Congratulations!" I said. "Good for you!"

"By the way," he said, "it's important that you know that Father James is the only one who knows why I'm here. All the rest think I had a nervous breakdown, instead of a LOVE BURST!" he shouted with joy.

We hugged again, holding each other a long time, then we continued walking along the lake together.

"Do you know where *Josefina* is?" I asked.

"I think so."

"Then you haven't been in contact with her?"

"Oh, no, like I said that's part of our deal, that we won't make contact with each other for six months."

I stopped walking and turned to face him. "Okay, all that sounds good and, well, reasonable," I said. "And yet, I hate to say this, but you can't trust these decision- makers of the Church, especially the higher and higher they get up in the politics of the Church." I took in a deep breath. "Has *Josefina* read *Rain of Gold?*" I asked.

He shook his head. "No, we'd never heard of you or any of your books. I only found out about you when I arrived here and I heard all these nuns talking so excited, about *Rain of Gold.*"

"Well, I really do suggest that you get a copy of *Rain* sent to her immediately. You see, I always tell young women that when they finally find a guy that they're really interested in to have him read *Rain of Gold*, and if he doesn't love the book to dump him, because *Rain* is all about strong women, and shows men and the whole world what it means to be a strong woman of substance through war, through peace, through all the twist and turns of life."

"And you think it will help *Josefina* not to lose faith?"

"Exactly," I said, "because they did everything they could to break the little nun that I'd proposed to, and I'm sure that they are now trying to do that to *Josefina*. My God, in just a few weeks Sister Theresa had aged years and lost so much weight it was frightening. I strongly recommend that you find out where *Josefina* is and send her a copy of *Rain of Gold*. But, "I added, "do not go through normal channels. Did she have any close nun friends?"

"Oh, yes, she was extremely loved."

"Well, then contact them. No, wait. Don't contact her best friend *Sophia*, I do believe. Contact her other best friend *Maria*."

"How do you know their names?" he asked.

"Look," I said, laughing, "once we get out of the prison of our limiting 5 sensory perception and we access our Kingdom of God with our Multi-Sensory Perception of our Full Natural 13 Senses, all of us then Know Everything! Truly, Jesus Knew what He was talking about when He said that we each have the Kingdom of God within us. Just think about it. Within the Kingdom of God is Everything, Past, Present, Future, and so then—"

"We Know Everything," he said, grinning.

"Exactly, but with 5 senses we don't have the tools with which to access all we Know deep inside of ourselves, and with our Full Natural 13 Senses, we do."

"Then this is how you Know what Einstein said about not riding on a beam of light, but that he became a Beam of Light?"

"Exactly," I said. "Albert is one of the Grand Masters that I'm now in contact with ever since my dad passed over. You see, when one of our loved ones passes over, we don't lose them. What actually happens is that we gain a stronger access to the Other Side of Living, and the Church used to acknowledge this until the 4th Century when they then decided to do away with reincarnation and all of our other Natural Knowledge that comes to us with our Multi-Sensory Perception."

"Then are you saying that you believe in reincarnation?"

"No, belief is a weak word, so I don't believe in anything anymore."

"I don't understand."

"Look, you don't believe that tomatoes taste good. You Know that tomatoes taste good. You don't believe in taking a crap. You Know you need to crap."

"Well, yes, but a tomato is something we can see and feel, and needing to crap is a function that our body tells us."

"Exactly," I said, "and once we move out of our prison of our limiting 5 senses, and into our Natural Multi-Sensory Perception of 13 Senses, then we stop believing and start Knowing with a capital K."

"Even God?"

"Most especially God," I said. "My two grandmothers didn't believe in God. They Knew God and they lived with the Almighty with their every Breath. But I also didn't fully understand this until I met two Native American educators in Nashville, Tennessee back in 1992 at the National Library Convention. And this is when I stopped believing and began to either Know something or not Know. Like I don't believe in God anymore, I Know God, and so just like my *mamagrandes* I, too, now live with the Almighty with my every Breath. And about reincarnation; no, I no longer believe in reincarnation. I Know reincarnation, here, deep inside of me."

"You know reincarnation?"

"Yes, I Know…that I've had 15 lifetimes on this planet and that this is only my second time as a male, and I also Know that I've had 1000s and 1000s of past lives on our other Six Sister Planets."

"Really? You Know this?"

"Yes, I absolutely Know this!"

"And you think, I mean, you Know that all of us can reach this Level of Knowingness?"

"Of course, we all have the Kingdom of God within us," I said.

He nodded and nodded again and said nothing more as we continued walking alongside the lake, listening to the little waves slapping up against the shoreline.

"You know," he said after a while, "these things you've been telling us are beginning to make sense, and I can now see they were in *Rain of Gold* between the lines, but I, well, hadn't been able to see them." He stopped, turned to me, and asked, "Did you do this deliberately."

"Oh, yes," I said, laughing. "After 265 rejections I Knew that I had to do what old Hemingway suggested and keep 7/8 of what I was saying under water or I'd never get published."

"I see, I see," he said. "You know what really resonated within me was when you said that our planet is a very emotional and sexual driven planet. I mean, ever since I admitted to myself that…that I was also physically in love with *Josefina* and not just spiritually, it's been so complete feeling within me that, well, I now see everything differently."

"Go on," I said.

"Well, it's like I now see everything alive and full of joy," he said, laughing. "I swear that when I first arrived here, the geese came rushing up to me and they congratulated me on being in love. I Know this sounds crazy, but it's true! That's what it felt like, and then the trees and the grass were all happy to see me, too!" He spun around, shouting with joy. "IT'S LIKE THE WHOLE WORLD KNOWS I'M IN LOVE AND IS SO BEAUTIFUL AND HAPPY FOR ME! And this is when I just KNEW that Jesus had been in love with Magdalene, and so, of course, they'd made love and had children! How could they not have, eh?"

I was laughing and laughing. "You're absolutely right, and they did have kids, and we'll get into all of that too, because this is, indeed, the most emotional and sensually driven planet and of our Six Sister Planets, and so it is our duty to live with all our Heart and Soul and Body and Mind, and this is how we finally have no Illusions of Separation and/or Mortality, and start Living on the Active Side of Eternity!"

"Then you believe–I mean, Know that believing is, well, in fact, misleading?"

"You tell me," I said. "You have your own Kingdom of God within you, and you're the one who's now in love, and with Love*Amor*, you are Totally Connected. You see, believing insinuates not Knowing, and as soon as you get people to not trust their Inner All-Knowingness, then this is when we become easy targets for manipulation by man- made institutions, because we've lost our Natural Direct Connection to God."

"I see," he said, nodding, "I see."

And once again he said nothing more and we continued walking and could see it in his eyes, he was letting all this soak in. This was a big one. To move from believing to Knowing had taken me years.

"Will you be talking to us about this?" he asked. "About Knowing?"

He nodded.

"You tell me," I said.

He laughed. "I think you should. NO, I KNOW YOU SHOULD! I'm sure a lot of us are tired of all the manipulation that was done to us!"

I burst out laughing with *carcajadas*. I liked this guy. I really did. I was so happy that he'd chased me down.

"Okay," I said. "I'll go for it!"

And it was now time for us to head back, so we could eat lunch. "So tell me," I said, "what is your relationship with Father James?"

"What do you mean by that?"

"Well, you two seem very close, so I was wondering if—"

"If we're gay? Yes, a lot of the others think that, but we're not," he said.

"Well, that wasn't what I was referring to," I said. "I was wondering if you Know that he's an Angel, actually a—"

"Oh, yes, I Know that," he said. "Of course, James is an Angel, if it wasn't for him I might have lost faith in my love."

"Then have you seen his glow?" I asked.

"Seen him glow? You mean, glow with Light like an actual Angel?"

"An Archangel," I said.

"Really? You're saying Father James is an Archangel?"

"Yes."

"Well, it doesn't surprise me," he said. "In fact, it actually makes sense. Without his help our good nuns would have never been able to bring you here. The priest, as I assume you've guessed, were not that keen to have you come."

It was my time to nod and nod again. "Oh, I see," I said. "I get it now."

"So how do you know that James is an Archangel? Have you seen others?" he asked.

"Yes, in Chicago I met this chubby *Latino* teacher, who looked a lot like the

Comic Paul Rodriguez, who was an Archangel."

"Really?"

"Yes."

"And what is the difference between an Angel and an Archangel? They're both God's Messengers of Light, correct?"

"Yes, you are right, and what I've seen," I said, "is that an Archangel's Light is almost as bright as the Golden Light I saw surrounding Jesus when He came to me in Spain."

"Really?"

"Well, maybe not that bright, but still highly illuminating."

"So, then, was your grandmother *Doña Margarita*, an Angel or was she an Archangel?"

I laughed. "Why do you ask that?"

"Well, the relationship that she had with the Virgin Mary, and the way Jesus would come to them in Church, but then she'd tell Jesus to keep still and not interrupt the conversation that she was having with His mother, made me think this."

I laughed again. "No, she wasn't really an Angel or an Archangel. She, like Walt Disney, Emerson, Einstein, Cervantes, and Confucius and Moses, was a Grand Master, and so this allowed her take on leadership, which Angels, and especially Archangels, are not allowed to do."

"Really?"

"Yes, that Archangel in Chicago explained all this to me. He was a high school teacher and I asked him if he was going to become a principal or a school district superintendent and really make a big difference in the Chicago school system, and he said no. That as an Archangel he could only illuminate but not lead and/or interfere, that we, humans, had to come into our own Enlightenment, and this was why Jesus hadn't brought down 10,000 Angels and destroyed the whole Roman Empire, but instead He'd given Illumination."

"I see, I see," said Mark. "And is this what your Great Great Great Great Great Aunt, Mothers Of No Specific Child, was doing when she allowed them to rape her and burned her at the stake?"

"Exactly," I said with tears coming to my eyes, "because she was Totally of Jesus, so she, too, could've brought forth all her Miraculous Healing Powers and the Heavens would've opened up with Legions of Angels but she chose not to do this just as Our Lord Jesus chose not to. And what They both did was Inspire us to Greatness! And Jose-Maria saw this, and so did many of the young soldiers."

"But the old priest couldn't see it," said Mark, "because he saw all the Native Americans as ignorant savages, and, well, I need to admit that I, too, can relate to that. When I first arrived in Ecuador I, too, couldn't see the purity of love for God that the local native people demonstrated so naturally. Then when I did, I began falling in love with *Josefina*. She and her fellow native nuns were just so pure in their love for God. Will you talk to us about this?" he asked.

"You tell me?" I said.

He laughed. "Well, I guess it will depend on our availability."

I laughed. "Exactly," I said. "I never Know what I'm going to do and/or say. My Spiritual Guides guide me moment by moment. And also I don't want those guys in the back to decide to burn me at that stake."

He laughed. "Well, anyway, when you said that this is a very emotional and sexual driven planet, then a lot of the feelings I've been having started to falling in place and – oh, I'm just looking forward to being married so much! I'm 40 years old and I'm a virgin! And I no longer want to be a virgin!"

"How old is *Josefina?*"

"She'll be 33 next week, and oh, boy, are we going to make babies!"

I put my arm around his shoulder. "Good for you! And I'd like you to Know that not just the geese and the trees and all of Creation here on our planet are rooting for you, but also Our Star Cousins from Our Six Sister Planets are rooting you, too. You see, Our Beloved Mother Earth is the Hawaii of our planets, and all Six Sisters are waiting for us to open up Our HeartEyes and SoulEyes with Love*Amor,* so that they can then flood us with MIRACULOUS HEALING POWERS!"

"OH, WOW! You're right! I can feel it! Because once I let myself fall totally wildly in love *con mi amor, Josefina,* then it was like the Heavens parted for me and I was so happy! And my Dreams became Adventures of Spirit like I'd been Reconnected Directly to Creation itself!

"Yes! Yes! Yes!" I said. "And it all begins with us allowing ourselves to fall madly unconditionally in Love*Amor!*"

"Yes, I can feel it! And this is exactly why *Josefina* and I will not allow anyone to make us feel ashamed of these wild feelings that we're feeling for each other!"

"Absolutely! Anytime, anywhere, any way two people fall in Love*Amor,* they are doing God's Holy Work on Mother Earth! Because only through Joy and Being Happy! BIG BIG HAPPY do we help the Almighty spread His/Her Love*Amor* throughout the WHOLE ENTIRE UNIVERSE!"

And saying this, I took Father Mark in my arms, and jerked him close, kissing him on one cheek and then on the other, and he didn't resist. In fact, he kissed me back on both cheeks, too. Then arm in arm the two of us continued up the grassy knoll through the honkers and deer and we could see there was a group of nuns and two priests waiting for us at the outside patio of the huge mansion. And they looked very excited to see us coming up the knoll. I guess that they'd been watching Mark and me. Coming into the patio, Sister Mary came rushing at me.

"I want one of those hugs, too!" she yelled, grabbing me in her arms.

And she hugged me with her whole body and then gave me a big long juicy kiss on each cheek.

"Oh, that was fun!" she said. "I haven't kissed like that since I was a teenager! And it felt wonderful back then, too!"

Margarita and two other nuns were in line and they, too, hugged me and kissed me, but not quite with the fire that Sister Mary had kissed me.

"How about you guys," I said to the two priests. "Come on, just a hug. We don't need to kiss."

One of the priests stepped forward. "I guess, I'll take a hug," he said.

And so we hugged, but he made sure to keep his lower body completely away from me, and then we all went inside to have lunch. And the honkers, they could feel the Love*Amor* that had come to us, and they now came honking up to the patio with great sound and excitement. Mark had been right. The birds, the trees, the grass, the lake, all of Creation could feel the Vibrational Frequency of our Love*Amor*!

BOOK TWO

SIX

A fter lunch I went to my room and took a little nap, and then when I awoke I was so happy! BIG BIG HAPPY that I'd listened to my mother and I'd come to see these old nuns and priest. I got up, washed my face, and went dancing down the hallway to the stairs.

"Thank You, God!" I said. "Thank You, Lord God! And thank you, *Mama*, and thank you, *Papa*! I'm ready! I'm all ready, so let's just go for it!"

And when I walked into the room where we were having our event, I saw that my dad and my brother Joseph and a whole bunch of other relatives and Grand Masters from the Spirit World were over by the windows facing the lake. I nodded to them and they all nodded back to me, and then Bossy Bill Shakespeare stepped forward.

"Oh, no, Bill," I said to him. "This isn't your show." Then I turned to Cervantes and said, "Please handle Bill for me. I don't want him trying to take over like he does."

"I could save you years of writing, if you'd just trust me," said Bossy Bill.

"Bill!" I said with authority. "We've been through this with you a dozen times! And I'm saying no to you now just like I said no to you 30 years ago in Ocean Beach!" "Excuse me," I heard someone say behind me, "but who are you talking to?"

I turned and saw that all the nuns and priests were staring at me, except Father James, who was smiling a smile full of mischief like saying, "Okay, *amigo*, now how are you going to get out of this one?"

And I Knew what he was talking about because I was fairly sure that only he and I could see these individuals from the Other Side of Living.

I took in a deep breath, and decided just to go for it all the way. "I'm talking to Bossy Bill Shakespeare," I said to the nuns and priests. "You see, ever since I took my oath to become a writer as great as Homer and/ or greater, Bossy Bill has been a pain in the ass, coming to me and insisting that he can help me to become a great writer. But I've always brushed him off, explaining to him that I prefer to get help from Cervantes, Azuela, Dostoyevsky, Tolstoy, and Anne Frank."

"But why would you refuse William Shakespeare's help if he is, in fact, coming to you and making himself available to you?" asked a priest.

I took in a deep breath and closed my eyes. "Because," I said, "when Bossy Bill Shakespeare wrote, 'To be or not to be' and he said that this was the question, he was barking up the right tree, but he'd missed the whole point, because to be or not to be is the answer. Not the question. And besides I find him to be arrogant and too much in his intellectual head and so I prefer Anne Frank who's centered in her heart."

I stopped. I could see that half of the nuns and priests were staring at me as if I'd just gone off the deep end. But then Father James saved the day. He started clapping vigorously!

"Wonderful!" he said. "Wonderful! And so should we put out more chairs? How many of these guests from Heaven are here with us?" he asked.

I had to smile. He really Knew his stuff. "Right now we have about a dozen," I said, "but I can see that others are coming."

"Well, we'll just put out two dozen more chairs," said Father James. "Tell me, are we going to be able to see them, too, I hope."

"Yes, I'm sure you will," I said, smiling, "especially after you sleep tonight, and tomorrow awake with the understanding that *mañana es,* indeed, *otro milagro de Dios,* that tomorrow is, indeed, another miracle from God."

Quickly, the priests and nuns brought out the other chairs and set them up, and this was when Father James came up to me and he was glowing.

"You're doing fine," he said to me quietly. "You're doing fine." "Thanks for the help," I said to him.

"That's what I'm here for," he said.

"Yes, I learned that in Chicago," I said. "All right, now continue," he said.

And he was in Full Illumination as he turned and went to sit down with the others. And this was when I Knew for sure that Mark and the other priests and nuns couldn't see Father James glow anymore than they could see our guests from the Spirit World. And yet all the nuns and priests were smiling and looking very happy. Yes, they could "feel" the Other Side of Living, but they couldn't "see" it until they'd Activated their Kingdom of God, and then to the degree that they allowed themselves to open up their HeartEyes and SoulEyes to this degree they'd Awaken.

"Okay," I said, "any questions?"

Our Spiritual Guests had taken their chairs along with the nuns and priests. Eight hands shot up.

"Okay, you in the back," I said.

"I thought we had free will," said this priest, "so then how can the Spirit World dictate to us?"

"You're right, we do have free will," I said, "but it's like choosing up teams to play baseball, and so once I made my deal with God up on that tall *mesa* out in the middle of nowhere in Wyoming, that was it. There is no turning back once you chose your team, because to choose, I'd put my whole Heart and Soul into our Deal, telling God if He didn't chicken-out on me, then I'd never chicken-out on Him."

"Just like Our Beloved Mother Teresa," said Mary with Holy Reverence as she made the sign of the cross over herself.

"Yes, exactly," I said, "and so 265 rejections was no big deal for me. My God, both of my grandmothers had suffered incredible starvation and gave witness to their children being slaughtered, so the deal I made with was FOREVER!" I added.

"And you were 19 years old when you made this deal with the Almighty?"

I wiped the tears out of my eyes. "Yes," I said, "I was 19 when I had that … that conversation with God, but then getting back home from Wyoming, it was like I'd lost that Inner Voice I'd heard so well out in the wilds. And this was when it came to me that I had to get away from *mi familia* and friends, who all thought I'd gone off the deep end, because they had absolutely no comprehension of what it meant to me to become a writer in partnership with God.

"Look, I'm also sure that the same thing happened to a lot of you with your friends and family who probably thought you'd lost it when you first informed them that you were going to become nuns and priests."

Many of the nuns and priest nodded.

"So what did you do to re-establish your conversation with God?" asked another priest.

I took in a big deep breath. "I decided to go six months without speaking, but to accomplish this, I also realized that I had to go to a place where no one knew me, and yet I wanted to stay close to the ocean, because *Nuestra Madre Pacifica* had always felt like my connection to God. So I rented a beach shack in Ocean Beach, and I was ready to go the rest of my life without speaking if need be, but then … then it was, I guess, somewhere in the middle of the 4th month when I was walking along the seashore late one night and the Heavens were full of Stars, that it came to me that it was, indeed, the darkness of the night that allowed us to see the stars.

"I stopped, I'll never forget, and I looked up at all the Stars, *mi familia*, as my *mamagrande* had taught me, and now, for the first time, I saw that the Darkness was Holy and so Beautiful because it was what gave Life to Stars! Tears came to my eyes, and I went back to my shack that night and I was listening to Sonny Rollins and his long pauses between the notes when it also came to me with such utter clarity that it was the Silence between the notes that gave Life to Music!

"I LEAPED UP SCREAMING! I'll never forget, I screamed and screamed and went running back to the beach, stripped off all my clothes, and went racing into the surf and the waves! For I could now clearly see that God had never stopped speaking to me! That He was, indeed, speaking to all of us through the Darkness of the Night that allowed us to see the Stars, *nuestra familia*, and He was also speaking to us through the Great Infinite Silence that gave Life to our Music!

"I swam out past the waves and I could now understand that God in His Infinite Wisdom had such Trust in me along with my Guardian Angel that He was Totally, Totally, Totally leaving it up to me to start making my own Holy Notes, my own Holy Music, for God needed us as much as we needed Him/Her so we could help plant His/Her ongoing Holy Sacred Garden here on Mother Earth just like my *mamagrande* HAD ALWAYS TOLD ME!

"And so, of course, it was that day at daybreak on the 16th of September 1960 with the Father Sun, the Right Eye of God, coming up with all His Glory that I started writing, and I've been writing ever since NON-STOP to this day some 40-some years later! And it was Sonny Rollins with his wondrous long pauses of Silence between his Notes that opened up the Heavens for me, and now all of *mi familia* and the Grand Masters began coming to me each morning at about 2 a.m. when I began to write. And everything was going fine and wonderful until ... until Bossy Bill tried to take over, promising me all these great riches. And I'm sure he was right, but not for me. Still Shakespeare was so insistent, that I finally quit arguing with him and just started putting up signs at the door of my writing room and in the kitchen that simply said, 'Keep Out, Bill!' "

"You really did that?" asked a nun, giggling with laughter. "Did what?" I asked.

"Put up signs that said, 'Keep Out, Bill!' "

"Oh, yes, sure, I had to. You can't fool around with the Spirit World." By now a lot of people were laughing.

But then one priest became very serious looking, and said, "Are you insinuating that William Shakespeare is an evil spirit?"

"Oh, no, not at all," I said. "Bill is fine and good, but just not for me. Look, just like you guys read in *Rain of Gold* that my grandmother *Doña Margarita* finally had to tell Jesus to keep still, because she was having a woman-to-woman conversation with His Mother, I had to do the same with Bossy Bill, or he would have taken over."

"Excuse me, but I'd assumed that scene with your grandmother was symbolism," said another priest.

"Oh, no, I don't write symbolism," I said. "I write stark raw reality within the perception of Our Full Natural 13 Senses."

"Will you explain this?"

"Yes, of course," I said, laughing, "but first let me tell you what happened a few years back when I shared this conversation about Bossy Bill with a bunch of university professors. After my talk an older black woman ran to get in the elevator with me and she was all smiles until the doors closed. Then she started screaming and hitting me with this huge book of the collective works of Bossy Bill, calling me all kinds of names. And she was strong and that book must've weighed half a ton, and I kept pushing buttons to try to get out of the elevator before she killed me.

"You see," I said, "English, the English language, has become a religion on its own, and has all but taken over the whole world, and Shakespeare's writing encourages this to such a degree that we now brag about "English Only" in our country, and this is not just dangerous, but self destructive because…because English is the only language that I know of that capitalizes the word 'I'. Spanish doesn't capitalize *'yo'* unless you're a California surfer and you drive a Toyota pickup and you block out the first two letters and the last two letters of the word Toyota on the back of your tailgate.

"And then add to this what I've already mentioned that only European based- languages have the word 'the' and you have a very arrogant self-serving language in English. Truly, everywhere I go I tell people that our only hope for this nation is to start learning other languages and not just European based, because now with modern brain scans we are beginning to understand that when you learn a second language you don't just learn more words. No, you actually start accessing other parts of the brain, and a third language causes flexibility of the brain and you then end up having a much better chance of not ending up with Alzheimer's.

"So I told this group of professors that Shakespeare was out-of-date and it was time for us to start learning African Languages, and Asian and Native American languages, and so this woman who was African, I'd thought she'd gotten into the elevator to congratulate me. Not kill me," I said, laughing. "And what I guess really pissed her off was when I'd said Shakespearian plays were also totally out-of-date, and what we needed was for *Roots* by Alex Haley to be made into a musical and/or a Broadway play every 10 or 15 years like they do for all these other American classics. Truly, it's no accident that even that African professor became enraged. Everywhere I now give talks, I find out that high school kids have never even heard of *Roots* and of Kunta Kinte being raised up to the Stars in that fantastic scene that still sends chills up and down my spine, because this was what was done to me by my *mamagrande!* Truly, we need to break loose from the prison of 'English Only'."

"That makes sense to me," said Father Mark. "It wasn't until I'd been down in Ecuador for nearly six months and spoke Spanish pretty well and also a good deal of the local Native language that I could begin to open my eyes and see that there is a whole world out there beyond English."

"Exactly," I said, "and even Bossy Bill is now beginning to acknowledge this, because he has become good friends with Alex Haley. In fact, they're now *compadres*."

"Oh, godfathers," said Mark.

"Yes," I said. "Look, the most important thing for all of us to remember on This Side and/or on the Other Side of Living is to Trust with a capital 'T', because we can't access the Kingdom of God that we have within us until we have the understanding and the Complete Trust that we live in a wonderful loving Universe. As Henry Miller so well said in his book *Tropic of Capricorn,* 'Once you give up the ghost everything follows with dead certainty, even in the midst of chaos,' then he took off in an Arthur Rimbaud- like journey."

Then one of our Spiritual Guests spoke up, but I didn't quite get what he'd said. And when he spoke again with his heavy Brooklyn accent, I laughed, because I now knew that it was Henry Miller himself, whom I'd once met at his home out at the Pacific Palisades near Malibu in Los Angeles.

"Okay, Mr. Miller," I now said. "I'm listening. Please, go ahead. Yes, of course, I hear you, and I was going to get into all that tomorrow, but not now. All right, all right, *papa*, I hear you, too."

"What's going on?" asked a priest.

"Well, Mr. Miller and my dad and now even Bossy Bill and Azuela are telling me to move you guys into Geniusing right now, and then I can start sharing with you the Eight Indigenous Concepts that will free us from the past, so then we automatically slipslide into World Harmony and Peace and Abundance for All as has already been done on our other Six Sister Planets. And they're also telling me to inform all of you that back at one time our Six Sister Planets were even more lost and violent than us, and so we can do this here on Mother Earth, because, remember, we, Human People, are Hollow Bones, Buffalo Bones, Holy Instruments for helping the Almighty spread His/Her Love*Amor* throughout the Universe!"

I took in a big deep breath. "Okay, fasten your seatbelts, because the first question we need to address before we can climb aboard Our Spaceship and BLAST OFF into Inner Outer Space is … is, are you a genius? Then after that the next question is how many of you can imagine, just imagine, the possibility of World Harmony and Peace and Abundance for All for the next 5,000 years, even with all the problems that we have going on. Ready? And if you can see it, if you can imagine it, then please raise up your hand for each of these two questions."

"You're joking, right?" said a priest.

"Oh, no, not at all," I said. "In fact, these two are the normal questions I ask everywhere I go, and I can now see that I shouldn't have let you guys off the hook and asked you these two questions right from the start. You see, when I ask kindergarten kids these questions, they immediately all raise their hands to both of these questions, and one little *vato*-kid in Texas even flipped on the floor and raised up both feet and both hands, and I said to him, 'So you think you're a genius, eh?'

"'Yes,' he said, 'I'm really good!'

"'What makes you think you're so good?' I asked.

"'Look at my finger painting,' he said.

"I walked over and looked, then said, 'That's as good as any Picasso!' "'Yes,' he said, 'because I'M A GENIUS!'

"'Okay,' I said, 'and since you're a genius, do you as a genius think we can have World Wide Harmony and Peace and Abundance for All for 5,000 years, even with all the *problemas* that we have going on?'

"'Sure,' he quickly said.

"'And why do you think this?'

"'Because it's MORE FUN!' he shouted."

And having shared this little story, I laughed and laughed, figuring that all the nuns and priests would laugh along with me, but they didn't. One priest immediately spoke up full of frustration.

"Yes, but that child had no idea what genius means or any comprehension of what it means to have world peace!" he said.

I closed my eyes. "And you do, eh?" I said. "Tell me, have you ever looked up the word 'genius' in the dictionary?"

"No, I haven't," he said.

I opened my eyes. "Well, then I'll tell you that kid in kindergarden knew more about genius than you do. For nearly 20 years I've been asking people these two questions and adults are all so quick to say that children don't know what genius means, and yet not once have I found any adult who has looked up the word and remembers what genius means.

"And this is no accident, because by first grade there are less geniuses, by second and third grade less and less, and by fourth grade there are no geniuses left, and then in the seventh grade the girls who get straight 'A's raise their hands and the boys who are bored stiff at school raise their hands sarcastically. You see, our educational system crushes genius and replaces it with kids who have learned how to cram for tests and regurgitate what they've been taught, and that's not genius.

"Okay, no more of this," I said, taking in a deep breath, "now let's just go for it like kinder-garden kids and have fun! BIG BIG FUN! Okay, ready? And so I now ask all of you here, who's a genius? Come on, go for it!"

Two nuns raised their hands.

"Okay, good, not bad," I said. "And I fully realized that all of you were educated to not brag, to not walk down the center of a hallway, but to walk along the edge of the hallway, so people wouldn't think that you are being arrogant, but... and this is a big 'but', being a genius, admitting to geniusing, isn't about arrogance. No, it's about Activating the Kingdom of God that Jesus so wisely told us is within each of us. So now come on! Go for it! Are you a genius?"

Still it was only the same two nuns who raised their hands. Henry Miller had been right. This question had certainly taken these old nuns and priests out of their comfort zone.

"COME ON!" I said again. "Once you give up the ghost, then all the illusions, all the fears and expectations and all the negative crap that's been fed to us since birth, dissolves, disappears, and then everything follows with wonderful dead certainty, even in the midst of chaos!"

Still no one else raised their hand.

"Excuse me," said the tall, elegant nun in the front row who'd said she'd been a mother superior, "but what is your definition of genius?"

I smiled. "Good question," I said. "Very good question. And I'd like you to know that I'm using the definition from Webster's New World American Language Dictionary of pre-1990, which states for genius: 'guardian deity, or spirit of a person; spirit, natural ability, and according to ancient Roman belief, a guardian spirit assigned to a person at birth.' Thank you, Sister, thank you very much.

"And you can now see that originally genius had nothing to do with being smart and/or having a high I.Q., and had everything to do with Spirit." I stopped and breathed so this could sink in. "In fact," I said, "this backs up what my *mamagrande* always told me about coming to this world with a Guardian Angel, and this is why I was raised up with the understanding that I was a genius, that we were all geniuses, because my *mamagrande* also told me that the corn had its own Guardian Angel, the string beans, too, and this was how the corn knew how to grow and what to do and the string beans also knew how to grow and what to do. So now that you can see that originally being a genius had nothing to do with arrogance, I.Q., and/or being smart, how many of you can now say 'I am a genius'?"

Three more nuns raised their hands.

"Good! Good! Excellent!" I said. "And now let me share a little story with you that I think will help all of us get over this hump of being overly educated."

And saying this, I walked back over to the podium and stretched out both arms, gripping the top of the grand old wooden structure and leaned on it as I continued.

"This happened a few years back in Florida when I was giving a talk to about 1,500 teachers and librarians," I said. "And at first, I'll tell you, I was also having to pull teeth to get them to say that they were geniuses, just as I'm having trouble now. But then I saw this young, very good-looking woman in her 30s in the 6th or 7th row to my right and she was crying. She just couldn't say it, and she really wanted to, and seeing this, it suddenly came to me what to do, and I asked the two women beside her to hug her, to give her love, and then once she'd calmed down, I asked this woman if she could please close her eyes and go back to a childhood memory before kindergarten when she'd been happy. She said she could and she closed her eyes, and I then asked her to see herself in a park having fun with her friends, or playing with a puppy, or by the seashore, or wherever, then I asked her if she was there, and she nodded yes. 'Good,' I said to her, 'very good, and now can this happy child say that she's a genius?'"

"Oh, you should have seen it, her whole face lit up with joy and she nodded yes, yes, yes! And so I then said, 'WELL, THEN SAY IT! Say 'I am a genius'. And she did, saying it with Power and Conviction and people applauded and some even had tears in their eyes, and I then had them all say it again and again! And COLLECTIVELY WE THEN EXPLODED! WE TRANSFORMED!

"And so now I want all of you here to STAND UP AND STRETCH! Because, you see, as I said earlier, this is a very emotionally and sensually driven planet, and so you need to feel it! And/or as my dad would always say when he'd have a drink or shake someone's hand, 'You got to feel it!' And so now I need for all of you to give each other a big hug! A big hug full of friendship and Love*Amor*. And yes, this also means you guys in the back. COME ON! IT WON'T HURT! Good! Good! Much better! And now I want all of you to close your eyes and go back to a happy day that you had before you started school. In the park. By the seashore. At a picnic. In the woods. Do you see this day? Just nod. Good! Good! And now that you're into this happy day with feelings of joy, and BIG BIG HAPPINESS! Can that little child within you say, 'I am a genius!'?"

The whole place now EXPLODED, too! And it was beautiful! Almost everyone was saying it, and I now Knew that Henry Miller had been an absolute genius to give me this guidance, because you COULD FEEL IT! Really feel it! All these old retired nuns and priests had LEAPED back into the happiness they'd had as a child! And so now, Collectively, we could move mountains! Tears of joy came to my eyes. WE'D DONE IT! We really had! We'd just traveled those 18 inches from the brain to the Heart*Corazon* and now we were really Hollow bones, Buffalo Bones, Human Being Instruments of God ready to spread His/Her Love*Amor* throughout the UNIVERSE!

"GOOD! GREAT!" I shouted. "And now that you're all once more officially kindergarten kids, how many of you can imagine World Harmony and Peace and Abundance for All for 5,000 years, even with all the destructive sick crap that's going on globally?"

All the nuns raised their hands and about half of the priests.

"Good! Good! Because, you see, the custom some Native American tribes of Central America have when you meet someone, especially a stranger, is to say, "Finally we meet, for you are another me, and I am another you.' Then they put their hands behind their back and touch their foreheads together."

"Which tribes are these?" asked Mark.

"I don't exactly know," I said, "this was first gifted to me by Mariano, my brother- in-law of my second successful marriage and divorce from his sister Juanita. But I assume that it's a greeting among many tribes. Juanita's mother is from Peru. Okay, now how are all of you feeling?"

"Wonderful!" said one nun, smiling with ecstasy. "Happy!" said another, with tears of joy.

And so the comments went on and on and then came a statement that stopped all of us.

"I can see them!" said a nun. "I can see our Spirit Guests, and I can see my … my own parents."

People were stunned. "Really?" asked several nuns.

"Oh, yes!" said this nun. "I'm back at that happy day as a child when we were all in the backyard of my grandmother's house and my parents are young and all of us kids have been given white, furry Easter bunnies."

"Real ones?" asked another nun.

"Yes, real rabbits! And their little hearts are beating so fast as we kids hold them and love them."

"We were once given real rabbits for Easter, too," said another nun. "And it was one of the happiest days of my life."

"And you loved to hug those rabbits, didn't you?" I said. "Oh, yes!" said the nun who was seeing the Spirit World.

"Yes," I said, "because, you see, to reach Spirit we also need to be anchored, and one of the most wonderful ways to feel anchored is to hug, especially when we sleep. Puppies all sleep rolled up together. Baby ducks and baby chicks cuddle up under their mother's wings."

"Just wait," said a priest to the nun who'd had her breakthrough, "are you telling us that you really see people in these empty chairs and that you just traveled back to your childhood and are with your young parents in your grandmother's backyard?"

"Yes, that's what I'm saying."

"But how can you be at all these places at once?"

"I don't know," said the nun, and we could see it in her face that she was losing sight of her Happy Vision.

I stepped in. "Sister," I said, "please don't try to explain anything to this Doubting Thomas. He's the problem! And he and his type have been the *problema* for the last 13,000 years! And all of you nuns please now hug our Visionary Sister, because, you see, it takes Love and Faith for us to open our HeartEyes and pass through the doors of the Garden of Eden that have opened up for her. Because we never, never, never lost the Holy Garden within, within our own Kingdom of God, and this is where we are all now going to go. No joke! We're on our way! And in the future any of you Doubting Thomases talk to me! Not to the ones who've just made their first breakthrough. But me, whose been going to the Garden through fire and storm for over 40 years and 265 rejections!" I was pissed. I needed a little break. "Okay. Let's take a 10-minute break, and then WE'RE GOING FOR IT! GOD BLESS US ALL!"

And saying this, I walked over and joined the nuns who were hugging our Visionary Sister. Father James came over and so did Mark, and our Love*Amor* Energy was so Powerful, that we Knew in Our Collective Heart*Corazon,* that we had just moved A MOUNTAIN OF FAITH AROUND OUR WHOLE BELOVED MOTHER EARTH!

SEVEN

I went to my room, washed my face, then I did something I hadn't done in years. Instead of just standing up and talking to God, I knelt alongside my bed, made the sign of the cross over myself, closed my eyes, and thanked the Holy Creator for His/Her Trust and Patience and Guidance and Understanding. And this felt so good that I got lightheaded and had to lie down and I was out like a light.

Then waking up, I felt so happy! BIG BIG HAPPY and ready to go, and looking at the clock on the bed stand, I could see that once more I'd only slept for eight minutes. I laughed. This was utterly amazing! And once again it felt like I'd had a full night's sleep! Then I went dancing down the stairs, and entering the room, I saw that not all of the priests had returned.

"Okay," I said, "I can see that not all of us came back, and that's okay, because now that we're all geniuses, we are going to start geniusing, and so we don't want any negative energy holding us back. Because, you see, once we are geniusing, then all of our *problemas* of the whole world disappear. No joke. They really, really do."

I glanced around and took in a deep breath. "All right, would anyone like to share what happened to them during our little break? Myself, I knelt down and gave thanks to the Almighty and got to feeling so good I became lightheaded and had to lie down, then when I woke up eight minutes later, I felt WONDERFUL! And still feel ABSOLUTELY WONDERFUL!"

A nun raised her hand.

"Yes?" I said.

"Well," she said with a huge smile, "I heard a voice speaking to me in Gaelic. And I haven't heard Gaelic since my family and I visited our relatives in Ireland when I was a young girl."

I smiled. "And how did that feel?"

"Wonderful! Exciting! The Gaelic language is so beautiful!"

"Yes!" I said. "And there's a reason for that. Gaelic is an Indigenous Language, not an empire-based language, and so it comes from the Heart and Soul and not just the Head, and so as Geniuses with the Gaelic language, we are now actually Jesusing, meaning that we are no longer just connected to our given nation and/or our country, but once more are Being Globally Directly Guided by God, by our Inner Voice, by our Guardian Angel, and we can now start to see things that we were never able to see before, and ... and this is when we realize that there are no such things as *problemas* here on planet earth, and once we realize this, then a WHOLE NEW UNIVERSE OF POSSIBILITIES OPEN UP FOR US!

"You see," I said, closing my eyes, "problems were deliberately created to siphon off Our Direct Spiritual Energies, so that we are then incapable of ever realizing who we, Human Beings, really are. Do you see what I'm driving at? Problems only exist because of opposing opinions. One group is for abortion, and another is against abortion. One group is saying that there is global warming and another group says there isn't global warming. And each opposing group uses all the facts they can assemble to back up their side of the argument, and the key words they use in European languages are 'the', 'or', and 'but', and these words don't even exist when we start Genius-Jesusing."

"Jesusing?" said a priest.

"Yes," I said, opening my eyes, "because Geniusing is, in fact, Jesusing for we are then Goding. Okay, no more please. Just fasten your seatbelts, because here we go! You see, right after *Rain of Gold* came out with Arte Publico from the University of Houston, I was invited to speak at the National Librarian Conference in Nashville, Tennessee. I was pretty nervous. This was my first big talk in years and I didn't want to blow it like I'd almost done with the English Teachers Conference back at Long Beach when my first book *Macho!* had come out. So I gave my little 15-minute talk about *Rain of Gold,* explaining that this book was so important to me that I'd asked my old mother to please mortgage her home so we could buy the rights back from Putnam in New York, because—I couldn't believe it—they 'd wanted to call if fiction!"

I stopped. I had to take in a big, deep breath before I could go on. "Then I explained to these librarians and teachers that books were Holy, that good books could take people out of their isolated existence and bring them together with Heart and Soul, and this was why every people, every culture needed their own Holy Voice and that *Rain of Gold* was the Holy Voice of my people, just like the Bible was the Holy Voice of the Jews, and Homer was the Holy Voice of the Greeks, and Confucius was the Holy Voice of the Chinese.

"Tears were running down my face by the time I finished my talk, so I went to the bathroom, figuring that I'd blown it and made a fool of myself, but then coming out of the bathroom I saw that most authors had three or four people waiting for them, but one author in the back had everyone in a huge long line waiting for him or her. I asked the tall, well-dressed guy, who'd come out of the bathroom with me, who was that author who had everyone. And he said that it was me. I was shocked. I had no idea what I'd said to cause this, and the place was supposed to close down at 11 p.m., but they had to keep it open until 1 a.m. in the morning, because the librarians and teachers kept demanding to see me. And all this time, as I was signing books and then pamphlets, because we'd run out of books, I'd noticed that there were two Native Americans squatted down over by a corner waiting for me. And after the last person was gone, they both got to their feet and came to me with huge smiles. One guy was real tall and the other was much shorter.

"'You did it, Brother,' said the shorter one. 'YOU KNOCKED THEM DEAD!' "'Yeah,' agreed the taller one with the huge wide shoulders, 'you really cleaned house!'

"'Yep,'" said the shorter one, 'you really got to the Whiteman's ear, and that's not an easy task to do.'

"But I didn't understand what they were saying, because I'd just given a little talk about my parents coming to the U.S. with their indigenous mothers from México. And I knew it was a good story, but so were the stories of these other writers. This was when the shorter one introduced himself, saying that he was Harry Walters from Arizona, and he was Navajo. Then the big one said he was Jack Big Shoulders from Montana and he was Lakota, then he teased how all the white women just couldn't stop kissing me and hugging me. And it was true. I must've gotten 500 kisses that night, but I still couldn't understand why my talk had touched these people so deeply.

"'You gave them Hope!' said the Navajo. "'You gave them Spirit!' said the Lakota.

"'Yes,' I'd said, 'but some of these other speakers were really good and had great stories filled with hope and spirit, too, and yet they hardly got anyone to come to their booths. So, why me?'

"I remember that the Navajo and the Lakota now looked at each other, and Harry said, 'Then you really don't understand what it is you did tonight?'

"I nodded, and this was when Jack Big Shoulders said, 'Brother, you just turned all of history on its ear, and you opened up doors the Whiteman has never seen open before, or at least not for the last 7,000 years!'

"'Exactly,' said Harry, 'you brought our native way of thinking and viewing the world right up in their faces and touched their hearts as they've never been touched.'

"'Look,' said the tall Lakota, 'the westward movement is over. They have no more continents to conquer, no more people to annihilate or enslave, and you just gave them a whole new world of possibilities!'

"'You see,' said the Navajo. 'when you said that every day is another miracle gifted to us by God, and that your Native American grandmothers taught you to give greetings every morning to Father

Sun, the Right Eye of God, and to watch Our Sister Corn smile her happy face and Our Sister Flowers open up with joy and Our Brother Birds begin to sing with Love*Amor*, you were giving people an understanding of Hope and Spirit and Love that touched their Hearts.

"'Then, when you added that the Mother Moon was the Left Eye of God and that the Stars were our Holy Family, because we were all Walking Stars, you tied everything together.' He smiled. 'Then when you added that we, Human People, also had Our Holy Sacred Work to do here on Mother Earth, just like Our Sister Corn and Brother String Beans, you gave meaning and purpose to every person's life in that room.'

"'In other words, you were giving the Whiteman back his Original Instructions,' the big Lakota told me, and he then explained to me that Whiteman had been lost for a very long time, and that they now didn't know where else to go or what to do, and I'd just opened a doorway for them to maybe return to their own Indigenous Roots.

"'You showed them,' he said, 'in a way that they could under-stand, that their ancestors weren't ignorant savages, but, in fact, were highly intelligent, well-thought-out, good people who'd lived in a sustainable way with nature.'

"'I did all that?' I'd said to them. 'But I just talked for 15 min-utes about my family.' "Hearing this, they both burst out laughing, and then they began to speak in Navajo or maybe in the Lakota lan-guage. I couldn't understand a single word they said, yet I kind of remembered, like in a dream, some of these throaty sounds and the use of tongue clicks that, I guess, I'd heard as a child from my Yaqui *mamagrande* and my uncle Archie, who had relatives out at the California Pala Indian Reservation. Then the two of them stopped talking to each other and turned back to me.

"'You tell him,' said the Navajo to the Lakota.

"'No, you tell it to him, Brother,' the Lakota said to the Navajo.

"'Okay,' replied Harry Walters, looking at me. 'We both believe maybe you don't really understand what it is you said tonight. And it's important you do, because obviously you will be speaking again, because you have reached the Whiteman's ear.'

"'Exactly,' said the Lakota. 'You got the Whiteman's attention, and that's a very difficult thing to do, Brother.'

"'You know,' I said, 'over and over my parents would tell me that I really didn't understand what it was they were telling me. My dad, in fact, finally said that I was *tapado,* meaning constipated in my head.'

"They both busted out laughing.

"'Your dad told it true,' said Jack Big Shoulders. "'Thanks,' I replied.

"'Let me try to explain to you what I think it was that your parents were trying to tell you,' said Harry.

"'Go ahead,' I said, glancing at the tall, muscular Lakota. He was all smiles. "'In the Navajo languaging,' continued Harry Walters, 'and in every native languaging that I know of, there is no concept of nouns. All there are is verbs.' "'So,' I said, 'what's that got to do with anything?'

"Hearing this, the Lakota burst out laughing again. "'Everything,' said the Navajo.

"'But how can that be?' I asked. 'A tree—that's a noun. It can't be a verb.'

"'Sure it can, because a tree is alive and always growing and changing through the seasons and through the years. It's *tree-ing,* a verb.'

"I gripped my forehead. 'Okay, but what about rocks? They don't change.' "'Yes, they do. If we lived to be ten million years old, we'd see that they are constantly changing, too.'

"'Oh, God, this is really confusing,' I said. 'But, well, didn't Einstein say that all there is, is change?'

"'Yes, he did, so he was doing it the Navajo way, just like you did it the Navajo way tonight.'

"'No, the Lakota way!' said the big man from Montana, still laughing.

"'All right,' I said, trying to figure out what they were saying, 'if everything is a verb, then do you believe in God?'

"'No, of course not,' said the Navajo, without batting an eye. 'That would be silly. We *do* God.'

"'You *do* God?' I said, gripping my forehead with both hands. Having been raised a Catholic, this was just so confusing that it hurt my head. 'But how in the world can you do God?' I asked. 'Hell—I mean, Heaven—we can't even agree on the concept of who or what god is.'

"'That's the whole point,' said the Lakota.

"'What's the point?' I said.

"'Why Native People have kept the Creator as a verb.'

"'Dammit,' I said, 'talk plain! You guys are killing me in my head!'

"'Years of constipation will have that effect on a man when he's finally trying to take a good mental shit,' said the Lakota, roaring with laughter.

But I didn't laugh. I was in terrible pain!

"'When we walk in Beauty, we are doing God,' continued Harry. 'When we are in Harmony with our surroundings, we are part of God. And when we find Peace within us, we are God.'

"'YOU ARE GOD!?!' I SHOUTED. 'No wonder the *padres* tried to slaughter all you savages! I mean, all of us savages! How in the hell—I mean, in Heaven—can we, human beings, be God?'

"'Easy. We are God as a verb, not as a noun. We are Goding once we find Peace inside of us,' the Navajo told me.

"'GODING!' I shouted with my whole head EXPLODING! I had to sit down. And the damn Lakota wouldn't stop laughing.

"'Dammit,' I finally said, 'I still don't get it! Goding? Goding? Are you then saying that it doesn't really matter what you think, and it only matters what you do?'

"'Now you're beginning to get it,' said the Lakota.

"'Well, if this is true, then it really doesn't matter if you are a Catholic, a...a Protestant, a Jew, a Muslim, a Buddhist, a born-again Christian, or even an atheist, because all that really matters is what you do, right? Not what you think or believe.'

"'Exactly!' said the Lakota.

"'Then we would have never, ever had any religious wars,' I said.
"'NOW YOU HAVE IT, BROTHER!' shouted the Lakota.

"'Then we've had all of our religious wars, not because of religion, but because of the language we use to do our talking and thinking about our religions.'

"'Now you really got it, Brother!' said the Navajo.

"'This is mind-boggling! IT CHANGES ALL OF HISTORY!' I shouted.

"'And this is exactly what you did tonight,' explained Harry. 'You changed the course of history!'

"'But how did I do this?' I asked.

"'You did it tonight,' replied the Navajo, 'when you said that your two Native American grandmothers didn't believe in God; they *lived* with God. You did it tonight when you said that your grandmothers didn't pray to God; they *spoke* to God. You did it tonight when you said God was their way of life, and you did it when you said that we're all Walking Stars and we came to Mother Earth with a Guardian Angel to plant the Stardust Seeds that we brought with us from the Heavens, and that God needed us as much as we needed God in order to plant His ongoing Sacred Garden. You totally changed the course of human history, because God was no longer perfect and unreachable, but instead close and very reachable.'

"I was stunned! They were right! I had said all this!

"'Yes, Brother, you had them eating out of your hand,' added the Lakota, 'and they were all ready to follow you anywhere, because in making God both male and female, you rolled back human history 13,000 years to the last ice age.'

"And I can tell you that those two guys kept talking to me, explaining my own book *Rain of Gold* to me, but I'd quit listening. I'd had it. They walked me to the elevator. They were staying across the way, where the rooms were more reasonable. The only reason I was staying at the hotel of the convention center was because my room had been paid for by the library association. And the big man from Montana was still talking, and I guess telling me something really important, but I just couldn't take it in. I was dead on my feet and I almost collapsed once I got into the elevator.

"And that night I had a flying dream and I was with my dad, shooting across the Heavens and this was when I realized that our Mother Earth really was no larger than a grain of sand on the Seashore of Creation and we, Human Beings, WERE SO HUGE that our arms and legs reached out to the furthest reaches of the Universe! God was a Verb and we were Verbs, too. Supreme Being was God and Human Beings were we. Both Being. Both Verbs.

"Okay," I now said, "all that happened to me in Nashville, Tennessee, but it really didn't register what all this verb stuff meant until about a month later when I was at the wrong hotel about 80 miles outside of Phoenix, Arizona, and the next morning I was scheduled to do a TV interview at 7 a.m. But there are no accidents, because being at this wrong hotel with the Heavens jampacked full of Stars was when it hit me with SUCH POWER what that Navajo and Lakota had been telling me as I'd gotten into the elevator that I went two years without sleeping! No joke! Just like Albert Einstein, I, too, became a Beam of Light!

"Ready? Because I now have a question for you Genius-Jesusing people that will also BURST YOU INTO BEING BEAMS OF LIGHT! Ready? Good. Good. And now close your eyes, and when you see the answer within your own Kingdom of God, I want you to raise up your hand, but please don't give the answer aloud.

"No, we need for over 50% of you to get this answer on your own, before we say it aloud. Because, like I said, when I realized the answer to this question I'm going to ask you, an Energy came BURSTING into me with such power that I really, really went two years without sleeping. And I then understood how my Great Great Great Great Great Aunt, Mother Of No Specific Child, had gotten to the age of 165 and how she could've gone on to the age 900 years, like Moses or Methuselah, in perfect health, because we, Human People, are, in fact, Living, Breathing Beams of Light! Okay, ready? Here is the question, but please just raise your hand. We need over

50% of you to get it on your own," I said, wetting my lips that had gone dry. "When did Creation happen if … if everything is a Verb?"

No one raised their hand.

"Come on," I said, "trees are tree-ing, rocks are rock-ing, and Albert Einstein proved that all there is is change."

One hand shot up. Then another and another. All three nuns.

"Good," I said. "We have three people who see it, and now I want you three to put your hands down and send your Love*Amor* to all the rest of our people, and I want you others to close your eyes and breathe in the Love*Amor* that is Being sent to you, because we're All, All, All Interconnected! And we're All, All, All Interplanetary Connected to the furthest reaches of the UNIVERSE!"

And this was when the priests who hadn't returned to our session now came quickly walking in and took their seats. One was a very big bulldog-looking guy. I guess that they'd been in the next room listening.

I laughed. "All right, and you guys who just came in, you, too, close your eyes, and breathe in deeply, and I ask all of you once again, when did Creation happen if everything is a Verb? Trees are tree-ing, rocks are rock-ing, and Einstein proved that all there is, is change. NOW GO FOR IT within your own Kingdom of God and raise your hands when you see it!"

Two more hands came up, but not with as much confidence as the first three.

"All right," I said, "now everyone open your eyes, and get up and stretch. We have about 25%, and what we need to happen is for all of us together to Circulate the Love*Amor* Energy that's shooting around us, so stretch! Stretch! And breathe deeply, then blow out fast! Yes! Yes! And do it a few more times. Good! Good! And now please take your seats again."

They did so.

"Great!" I said. "And so now tell me, when did Creation happen if everything is a Verb?"

Six more hands shot up, and these came up with energy and confidence.

'WONDERFUL!" I shouted. "WE DID IT! We got well over 50%! So tell it! Speak it! Verbalize it! When did Creation happen if everything is a Verb?"

"RIGHT NOW!" shouted one of the nuns who'd first raised her hand. "ALWAYS!" shouted another nun.

"It's still happening!" said a priest.

"It has never ceased happening!" said another priest.

"It's ongoing forever!" said several people at once.

"YES! YES!" I shouted. "You're all right! So you see, we didn't get left out of the Super Bowl! And that guy in the wheelchair doesn't get it, because he's stuck in nouns and in five senses, because there are no beginnings and ends! IT'S STILL BANGING! Right Here! Right Now! Forever! And Ever! So how does this feel?"

"I think it's mind boggling," said a priest.

"Well, then, stop thinking. Because all thinking is done with manmade words and manmade words are limiting within their own definition, and so we need to get into our feelings, our Knowingness, which is INFINITE! So I ask again, how does this FEEL?"

"Look," said the same priest, "this is still too new for me to think about it."

I laughed. "So stop thinking! You see, what happened is that nouns are one of the things that we ate from the Tree of Knowledge, and with nouns we solidified creation, and then we imposed our manmade concept on Creation. We said, this empire started here and ended there. This king started ruling here and his ruling ended here. And we then took our idea of beginnings and endings and imposed them on nature. So can you now begin to see, to feel, to glimpse that the doors of the Garden of Eden are re-opening? Eh, can you glimpse this?"

All the nuns nodded and several of the priests nodded, too.

"Good, good," I said, "and now that you can clearly begin to see that Creation is ongoing, tell me what happened to the old concept of death? Go ahead. Talk it, speak it, put it in words right now!"

"It ... it disappears," said a nun, with her eyes getting huge.

"It never existed," said another nun in astonishment.

"Then we're always dying and living," said a priest.

"I read somewhere that every seven years all the cells of our bodies renew, so that infers that the old ones died," said a priest.

"Oh, my Lord God," said another nun, "then this is what you were referring to when you said that once we Activate the Kingdom of God within us, we begin Living on the Active Side of Eternity!"

I nodded. "Yes, exactly," I said, with tears of joy were streaming down my face. "And now that we have slipped out of the two old concepts of nouns and death that have been holding us back, and we see that Genius-Jesusing and Creation have always been ongoing, now I'd like to ask you who … who are we in Full Partnership with?"

"WITH GOD!" shouted a nun.

"With Creation!" said another nun.

"And so we now no longer believe in God, but live with God," said another nun, "just as your grandmothers were living with Our Holy Creator."

"Exactly," I said. "And so how does this feel?" "FANTASTIC!" yelled a nun, leaping to her feet. "WONDERFUL!" shouted another nun.

"For the first time in my life I can love God without fear," said another nun with tears pouring down her face.

"Can't talk," said Margret. "Too beautiful! Too beautiful!" And she also had tears of joy running down her beautiful, elegant face.

"WE NEED TO TELL THE POPE!" shouted a priest from the back. "This can REVOLUTIONIZE OUR WHOLE CHURCH!"

"DIDN'T YOU HEAR HIM?" yelled Mary. "The Pope is a man! And over and over he's told us that it's now women who are going to lead! And men need to listen and 'follow infront'!"

"Well, yes, but maybe it can help," said the priest, sounding defensive.

"How can it help?" said Mary. "What we need is a woman Pope!"

"A woman Pope?" said several priests at the same time.

I raised my hand, closing my eyes.

"Yes," I said, "Mary is right. We are going to have a Woman Pope," I opened my eyes and breathed deeply. "And Our First Woman Pope will happen when... when the Vatican moves to Ireland."

"Then you think the Vatican is really moving to Ireland," said several people. "Yes," I said, "and you, who said that we need to tell the Pope, are also correct, but it's our next Pope that we need to tell, because it will be our next Pope who will set the stage for Our First Lady Pope and our movement to Ireland." I closed my eyes, smiling. "He'll be dressed all in white and will be our big strong male Snow Goose Pope 'following infront' across the Father Sky as big strong male geese have been doing for over 20 million years for this is, indeed, an intricate part of Our Human Being Ongoing Collective Godelution.

"Go on," I said, "all of you just close your eyes, place both hands over your Heart, and see-feel that you already Know all this in a Cellular Level deep within yourselves, and tonight you will start accessing all this in your sleep. Remember," I added, "what ever we can imagine, and then put Our Heart and Soul Energy into, becomes our Reality."

"YES!" shouted Mary, opening her eyes. "Then that's why this beautiful voice sang to me in Gaelic last night! Oh, it's true!" she said, turning to everyone. "The whole sky was full of Angels singing in Gaelic! Have you ever heard Gaelic? It really can't be spoken. It needs to be sung, because it sounds like Heaven, just like Enya."

"You dreamed all this last night?" asked someone.

"It was more than just a dream," she said. "It was more like, well, a –"

"A VoyageDream," I said. "I real actual happening, and all of you will now start experiencing VoyageDreams as you go slip-sliding into Our Collective Multi-Sensory Perception. For truly, you are now in Full Partnership with God-Goding Creation. In other words, like my grandmother always used to tell me, God needs us as much as we need God for Creating Heaven here on Mother Earth."

"THAT'S IT!" shouted Mary. "I truly felt like I was, well, in Partnership with God, and so this wasn't just a dream at all! But something that has—how can I say it—has already happened. Can that be right?" she asked.

"Of course," I said. "Just close your eyes again, and breathe, breathe deeply, letting go of everything you think you know, and get into your feelings, your intuition here within your Kingdom of God."

Mary closed her eyes, breathing deeply.

"Good, good," I said. "You see, only when we are totally relaxed can the Spirit World to come to us. You are doing very well, Mary, and . . . and don't worry about contradictions or sounding ridiculous. Remember, man-made words are shallow, one- dimensional, and have only been around for 30,000 years at best, and singing, chanting, drumming, dancing around the fire has been with us for 100s of 1,000s of years, if not millions, and this is exactly why the Vatican is moving to Ireland for 100 years and going to make the Native Language of Gaelic Her Official Language, instead of the dead, non-changing language of Latin. And then after Ireland, the Vatican will move to México for 100 years and once more take on another non-empire based Native Language, then move to the Philippines for a 100 years and take on another Native languaging, and then come back to Europe at a rich valley between France and Germany for 100 years and take on the pre-Roman Native languaging, then shoot down to Africa, zigzagging from Africa and the Americas and Asia and all around the world every 100 years for the next 50,000 years, becoming truly Catholic!"

"AND CATHOLIC MEANS UNIVERSAL!" shouted the big burly bulldog-looking priest.

"Yes," I said, "that's what we Catholics are always told. But have you ever looked up the word 'catholic' in the dictionary?"

He shook his head.

"Well, Father—"

"Joe," he said, "just call me Joe."

"Well, Joe, I suggest you look up the word 'catholic' and you'll find that the definition doesn't end with 'universal'. The full definition, according to the pre-1990 Webster New World American Language Dictionary is 'universal, all inclusive, of general interest and value, having broad sympathies and understanding; hence, liberal'."

They were stunned.

"Yes, I, too, was shocked," I said, "when I looked up the word 'catholic', and … and now I'd like for you to consider what Bishop Malachy from Ireland said in the 12th century."

"He said that we'd have 112 more Popes," said Joe.

"And our next Pope will be number 112, and he'll be our first Pope from the Americas and a Jesuit just like my brilliant ex-Jesuit *amigo* Greg from Chicago, and he'll set us up for Our First Official Woman Pope just as Jesus let me Know when he gifted me His Holy Sacred Heart*Corazon* in Madrid, Spain back in 1992. And all of you … all of you already Know All This Deep Within Our Own COLLECTIVE CELLULAR MEMORY!"

I stopped.

I took in a deep breath and blew out fast. They were all staring at me, so I closed my eyes and just kept breathing in deeply and blowing out fast.

"HOGWASH!" yelled Joe. "Bishop Malachy wasn't correct about everything, you know!"

"It's not hogwash!" snapped Mary. "Since everything is a Verb and we are then all in Full Partnership with God, how can we then not Know this to be true within Our Own Kingdom of God!"

This was a brilliant answer, but I could also see it wasn't quite satisfying Joe and the other priests.

"Joe, I suggest you just go back to that place within yourself," said Margret, "when he asked us to consider how would we all be today if Peter would have not looked down, and he would have instead walked on water alongside Our Lord Jesus. And I, then, do believe that you won't even be arguing with Mr. Villaseñor."

"She's right!" said another nun. "And you priests didn't help raise the money to have Mr. Villaseñor come to see us, so I say, SHUT UP! Or please leave so we can continue this Enlightening Event! A WOMAN POPE!" she added, with tears of joy coming to her eyes. "It makes Total Sense, especially since we are finishing up 26,000 years of out-of-balance Male Energy and going into 26,000 years of Balanced Compassionate Feminine Energy!"

Two priests got to their feet, looking all upset. I guess for being told to shut up by a nun.

"OH, SIT DOWN!" shouted Mary. "You guys are too old to revolt, and besides, it's us, the nuns, who fix your food and do your laundry, so just get off your high and mighty crap, and SIT BACK DOWN!"

The two old priests sat back down, and the nuns started laughing with such *gusto* that I couldn't help it, and I started laughing, too.

EIGHT

We broke for dinner and I went into the large bathroom just off the main dining room where we were scheduled to dine in the evening. It was a huge, ornate beautiful bathroom and I'd just unzipped and was starting to take a pee, when the door suddenly opened behind me with a bang and there stood Joe, the big burly priest and his face was all red with rage.

"MY GOD!" he shouted. "YOU JUST DON'T STOP!"

"Excuse me," I said, "but I'm trying to pee!"

"SO PISS! NO ONE'S HOLDING YOU BACK!"

And saying this, he turned and closed the bathroom door, locking it, and then came walking towards me. I suddenly didn't need to pee anymore. This huge man outweighed me by a good 80 pounds and it didn't look like he carried much fat, so even with all my knowledge of having been a wrestler and having been trained in advanced boot camp in the Army, I figured that I really had very little chance to defend myself against this huge guy in such close quarters.

"I need to speak with you!" he said, gasping for air.

"Well, okay, good," I said, "but could we do it outside on the grass by the lake after I pee?"

"NO!" he shouted. "This needs to private! Pee! I'll wait!"

"In here with me?"

"YES!"

"Well, okay, but I don't think I can pee with you watching," I said.

"All right, then you can pee afterward, and I'll just tell you what I need to tell you right now," he said.

"Okay," I said, glancing around to see if there was any chance of escape. "I'm a cross-dresser!" he said.

"You're a what?" I said.

"You heard me, A CROSS-DRESSER, DAMNIT!"

"Okay," I said, "but, well, you see, I need a little help. I don't exactly know what that means. Are you telling me that you're gay?"

"NO, I'M NOT GAY!" he barked. "I'm straight! This has nothing to do with being gay! You see, I was raised by my mother, a big woman, and I'd see her put on her make up and get all dolled up to go to bars to find a man for the night, and well, it angered me that I wasn't enough for my mom, but then once, when she was gone, I sat down before her mirror and I began putting on makeup like I'd been watching her do for years, and it calmed me down, especially when I looked at myself in the mirror and saw an attractive young woman. So, well, after that, I then began doing it every time she went out, and I became a big kid, so by 14 I was able to fill out her dresses, and this was when she once brought home this man who was abusive to her, I … I, well, literally BEAT THE LIVING SHIT OUT OF HIM and threw him out, and I guess she thought I was one of her girlfriends, so she thanked me and then in the morning she thought it had all been a dream."

"So then, you were dressed like a woman when you beat the crap out of that man and threw him out?" I asked.

"YES! OF COURSE! THAT'S THE WHOLE POINT! As a man I've never beat the hell out of anyone, but dressed like a woman, I've … I've, well, brought many situations to justice, and then when I became a chaplain attached to the U.S. Marines and some of our G.I.s would confess to me the horrible things they'd do, not just in war, but at home with their own families, I'd go to my place afterwards and put on makeup and get all dolled up and, forgive me God, but dressed as a woman I would go find these Marines and I'd beat the living crap out of them, and THEN I COULD FORGIVE THEM!" he yelled and then took in a huge deep breath and blew out fast. "Do you now see what I'm talking about? As a woman I can forgive, BUT NOT AS A MAN!"

It was me who now took in a great big deep breath. I had absolutely no idea how to respond to this, and here I'd figured that this great big tough-looking guy had probably abused altar boys and maybe even other priests. Never had it crossed my mind that he'd dressed up like a woman and defended women. Then I laughed. I mean, he'd had to have looked pretty attractive to have lured those Marines in so close.

"You're pretty big," I said, laughing. "So it must've been pretty difficult to find attractive dresses large enough to fit you!"

He started laughing, too. "It was," he said, "so I had to learn how to make alterations."

"And only as a woman have you beat the crap out of men?"

"Yes, that's true," he said. "Only as a woman, and this is why I had to see you privately."

"But not to beat me, right?" I said. "Because you're dressed like a man."

"Oh, no," he said, "I came to tell you how wonderful it is to hear all the things that you're telling us, because then, maybe, I'm ... I'm not going to go to hell and burn for eternity when I die," he said with tears suddenly coming to his eyes. "Because revenge and not forgiveness I can now see is what I did for most of my life as, well, supposedly, a man of God."

I took in another great big deep breath and blew out fast. My God, my God, my God, then this big tough-looking man had truly been paying attention to all I'd said.

"You know," I said, "I can now see that you were really taking in all that I've been talking about, and here I'd thought you were really just being sarcastic."

"Oh, no, not at all," he said. "It's quite the opposite. I ... I, well, saw you levitate."

"Leva-what?"

"Levitate, rise up off the floor."

"You saw me do that?" I said, swallowing. This frightened me. Only once before had anyone ever said that they'd seen me do this.

"Yes, when you repeated the words 'I am a genius' over and over again, then you made the connection that Geniusing was, in fact, Jesusing, at that point you levitated and Prince saw it, too."

"Prince?"

"Yes, that's what we call Father James, because he was the chaplain in Washington, D.C. and all those high and mighty came to confess to him. He and Margret both saw you levitate. You're not alone, Mr. Villaseñor," he added. "Some of us have had experiences that aren't too much different than your own."

Once more I took in a deep breath, and I flashed on the Archangel I'd met in Chicago, then I flashed on the L.A. rush hour traffic parting for me like the Red Sea, then I flashed on the realization that I really wasn't alone and so none of these Miracles and even Levitating were really me. No, they were simply proof that we were All, All, All Interconnected with Creation Creating, and that there were others all over our planet who were also already coming forward and stepping up to the plate in preparation for this shift that would happen on December 21, 2012, so Collectively we could help plant Our Stardust Seeds in profusion until November 10, 2026 at 3pm California time.

"Okay," I said to him, "I think I can piss now."

"Do you want me to leave?" he asked.

"No, you might as well stay," I said. "My God, a cross-dresser and a Chaplain attached to the Marines. Wow! What a life you've lived!"

"That's not all of it," he said.

I turned my back on him, unzipped again, and began to pee.

"You should talk to Prince," he said. "He's the one who's really had the life, hearing the confessions of all those movers and shakers in Washington D.C. Those confessions make the atrocities that I heard from our fighting boys sound like child's play. You're dad was right, our whole damn world really is upside down and stupid, and don't you think for a minute that the Church isn't still asking us to sprinkle holy water on the atrocities that She allows our good Christian soldiers to commit, and then has us say the equivalent to these service men that they only killed their earthly bodies, but they saved their immortal souls for the love of God and the honor of the United States.

"And these young men believe us, because we're priests, and I used to believe too, until now that I've been retired, and for these last 15 years I've had a chance to reflect. Truly, I now believe that more of us of the cloth are going to go to hell when we die than regular people, because we out-Nixoned Nixon. Watergate was nothing compared to what we've been hiding for centuries."

"And yet you were still able to see me levitate," I said. "And I've only had one other person ever tell me that she saw me levitate. It was a woman healer from Carlsbad who self-published a book about healing yourself."

"Carlsbad, New México?"

"No, Carlsbad, California, and as I'm sure you know, only a very Spiritually Elevated Human Soul can see levitation, so I'm sure that you're not going to hell," I added.

"How can I not be? Judgment Day is just around the corner and that's the Day when Jesus is returning to—"

"No," I said, "it's not coming."

"Judgment Day isn't coming?" he asked.

"No, it's already here. And Judgment Day is the day when we all stop passing judgment on each other, and especially on ourselves."

He looked all confused.

"Didn't Jesus say to forgive them for they did not know?" I said.

"Well, yes, He did, but—"

"There are no 'buts' in life," I said, "because you're also part of the package that doesn't know. Stop being so full of self-importance that you think you're superior to those who drove the nails into Our Lord Jesus' flesh. You are every bit as ignorant as they were. In fact, if Jesus were to come to us right now today, who do you think would be the first ones to want to do Him in?"

"I don't know," he said.

"Come on," I said, pissing. "You know. Tell me who's all full of judgment."

"Well, I guess you're pointing at my fellow Christians," he said.

"Exactly," I said. "It is us, you and me and all our most conservative and self- righteous Christians, who'd drive the first nails into Our Lord Jesus if He was to come to us once again."

"Unless He came dressed in fire and damnation!" he added, laughing. "Yeah, I guess you're right. Then you really do think that I'm part of those who didn't know, and so I can be forgiven?"

"Absolutely," I said, "because once we truly open our eyes to the full Glory of God, then we can only do the Sacred Holy Good, and your eyes are just beginning to open now that you're retired and have had time to reflect."

"Then I really am forgivable," he said, with tears coming to his eyes.

"Yes, of course," I said, taking in another deep breath. "You are a good man, Joe. A very good man, and I bet you make a pretty good-looking big girl, too," I added, laughing.

He burst out laughing, too. "It's true," he said. "I watched my mother put on her makeup for all those years and get all dolled up and I'd see this large pretty homely looking woman, totally transform. So you're right, I must say, I did look pretty snazzy when I was young and I'd get myself all dolled up."

I walked across the room and washed my hands after I'd finished pissing. "Has anyone ever seen you?"

"You mean dressed as a woman?"

"Yes."

He became as embarrassed as a little girl. "Prince. He saw me once. But no one else."

"What is it about Prince?" I asked, drying my hands. "It seems like a lot of people entrust him with their darkest—no, not darkest, but their most exciting secrets!"

He yelped. "That's it! That's it! It's because he, too, manages to do what you just did. We tell him our darkest secret, and he gives our secret back to us in Light and Joy, and we then feel totally better about ourselves, and this was what he did with those big-shot movers and shakers in Washington. They all adored him!"

"Yes, and Father James is able to do this, because he's an Archangel," I said.

"Prince is an Archangel?"

"Yes."

"You know, that makes sense," said Joe. "And he's the one who convinced us priests that it was okay for the Sisters to invite you to come and see us."

I nodded, then said, "Okay, and I now need to know how you'd like for us to go out of this bathroom. Do I go out first and you stay here for a couple of minutes, or do we just say to hell with it and go out together arm in arm?"

He looked at me. "You're right," he said, "this is a delicate situation, so, well, maybe we shouldn't go out together," he added. "But I also saw that you didn't have any trouble hugging and kissing Margret."

"Hey, do I detect a little jealousy?" I said, smiling.

"You're damn right!" he said. "I've been in love with that woman for over 60 years, and I've never so much as held her hand, and here you were hugging her and then kissing her. And Sister Mary, too!"

"You've been in love with Margret for over 60 years?"

"Yes, of course! I'm a priest, but also I'm a man!" he said. "And she's the most beautiful and wonderful woman I've ever met!"

"Well, then why haven't you hugged and kissed her?" I asked.

He broke down crying.

"Is it because you're a priest?" I said. "You know, there are priests who have fallen in love and left the priesthood."

"Yes, of course, I know," he said. "And I've considered that, but then I have to admit to myself that being a priest isn't really what has held me back. What has held me back is that I don't even know how to talk to a woman, and especially not about such feelings like love. And yet I've tried, but then I get all nervous. I'm 85 years old, and—"

"You're 85!" I said. "Hell, I'd thought you were in your late 60s or early 70s!"

"No, I'm 85, and I've never been with a ... a woman or a man. Sometimes I think these gay priests have it made. They get to have an intimacy I've never experienced."

I had to take in several deep breaths. Wow! Never in 100 million years had I ever expected any of this.

"May I hug you?" I said.

"I thought you'd never ask," he said, opening up his arms and coming to me, and it was a good thing that I'm strong and in great shape, because the bear-like hug he got me in could've broken ribs.

And so we held each other for a long time, and then I finally pulled away.

"Hey, but you kissed her!" he said. "We all saw you kissing Margret!"

"Okay, okay," I said. "I'll kiss you, too."

And so I kissed him on the right cheek and then the left cheek.

"My dad never even kissed me," he said, wiping tears out of his eyes. "Thank you. I'm in my 80s and this is my first real hug and kiss!"

"Wow!" I said.

And so we looked at each other one last time, smiled, and then we turned and just went out of the bathroom together arm in arm, laughing with *carcajadas*.

"You know, Joe," I said to him once we were walking down the hallway, "when I was hugging *Margarita*, she told me that she hadn't been hugged by a man since her dad last hugged her when she'd been 18 years old, and she's now 91."

He took in a big deep breath. "Then you think," he said, "that she'd be open for me to take her hand and ask her for a hug?"

"Absolutely!" I said. "You're a big strong handsome-looking man." "Really?"

"Yes, and you don't need to get dolled up," I added.

"Hey, that's confidential! Please, not one word!"

People looked at us as we walked down the hallway, but it seemed like they really didn't care and/or even made the connection that we'd just come out of the bathroom together. They were just happy to see us happy.

I was thirsty. I decided to get a glass of water, and then drink some wine before dinner. Wow! This encounter with Joe had just TOTALLY BLOWN ME AWAY!

NINE

"All right," I said, "we've just had a wonderful, relaxing dinner, and so I'd like for us to keep this good relaxing feeling before we turn in for the night." I took in a great big deep breath, and as usual it caused most people to take in a deep breath along with me. "And I'm very proud of us," I continued, "for having gotten as far as we have. This is all major stuff. Myself, it's taken me years and years to truly comprehend these things I've shared with you today, and many of you, well, got it so quickly."

A priest raised his hand. We were still in the dining room, sitting at our different tables and sipping coffee, but I didn't drink coffee. If I did, it would keep me up all night.

"Yes," I said.

"Did you really mean it when you said that you went two years without sleeping?" "Yes, I really meant that."

"But that seems totally impossible! You must have slept!" he added.

"Ask your guides, ask your Guardian Angel tonight to help you with this, and then tell us all about it tomorrow. Because I agree with you, it does seem totally impossible, but walking off a cliff seemed impossible, too, and parting L.A. rush hour traffic, and yet all those are true, too."

"And not just a dream?" he asked.

I took in a deep breath. How could I handle this, because all of Living Life, *la Vida,* was a DreamVoyage. Then it hit me.

"Look," I said, "I wasn't going to get into this tonight, and yet I now believe—I mean, I now feel and am also being told that I should get into this right now. You see, in *Oaxaca, México* before the European people came, it was recognized that we have three centers, not one, for processing information. One center is the Brain Computer and it has 4 Senses, all located at the head: sight, hearing, smelling, and tasting. Specific information from specific location. Another center is the Heart Computer and it has 3 Senses: feeling, balance, and intuition, and these three are done with our whole body. We feel 26 arms-length in all directions. Have you ever walked into a room and instantly felt something was wrong? Of course you have. We all have. What you did was feel 26 arms-length in all directions with your whole body, and if it all felt balanced, then everything was okay. But if something was out of balance, you instinctively, intuitively, you knew something was wrong.

"And … and you knew this with a capital 'K'. You didn't think this. You Knew this and Knowing is 100s of 1000s of years old, whereas our thinking with manmade words is only, at best, maybe 40,000 years old. So thinking is to the Brain Center as intuition and/or the Voice of Genius is to the Heart Center.

"All right, got that? Good. Good. And now we can move into our third center for processing information, and this is the Soul Computer, here in our gut, and this one has 6 Senses. The first of these is Music, the 8th Sense, because when God Created the Universe, He/She Created One United Verse, One United Song, and each of us comes into manifestation with our own Song, and then once we move into this computer, then Time and Space, our 9th and 10th Senses, are relative, as Einstein said, and/or they simply disappear, and we now move into our 11th Sense, which is our Collective Consciousness of All the Past and of All the Future, and we now have—"

"Psychic powers like Bishop Malachy of Ireland!" said the priest who'd said all this was impossible."

"Exactly!" I said. "Because Psychic is to the Soul as Intuition is to the Heart and Thinking is to the Brain!"

"Oh, wow! Then not sleeping for two years is possible!"

"Exactly!" I said. "Because we become Beams of Light just like Albert Einstein, and Light needs no sleep, and it doesn't age, either."

"I see, I see," said the priest, "then everything you've been sharing with us all day is the norm once we Activate our Kingdom of God with our 13 Senses. But what is the 13th Sense?"

"Being," I said. "Supreme Being and Human Being, and this is when we are at One with Goding."

"It's making sense now!" he said. "This is wonderful! And so when I go to sleep tonight, and I stop all of my thinking with manmade words, I'll then be, through feelings, in Direct Communications with God!"

"Exactly," I said. "And now that most of you here are 78 and/ or older, please ask tonight for your Blessed Tools with which to become a Sacred Elder. This is one of the main things we're missing in our whole western civilization. We worship youth," I added. "And I love that I'm getting old!"

"ME, TOO!" yelled Joe. "Anymore questions?" I asked.

"Yes," said a nun. "Why did you refer to the word 'the' so many times?"

"Oh, wow!" I said, taking in a deep breath. "This is a big one. You see, the word 'the' only exists in European-based languages. The Russian language doesn't have it. No Asian language has it. No Indigenous language has it. Only Europe, and it was invented by the Jews and their cousins, and then popularized by the Greeks, and then all of Europe adopted it. And I'm not bad-mouthing the Jews or the Greeks. My ex-wife is Jewish. My two sons are Jewish. And I'm Jewish through digestion. And at first the word 'the' is innocent sounding, because you use it to say 'the tree' in front of my house. "And the rest of the world has 'that tree' and 'this tree' to show location. Only Europe has 'the tree', but then European people jump from 'the tree' to 'the truth' and what happens to truth? Go on, tell me what happens to truth when you place 'the' in front of it? Come on, you're all geniuses."

No one said a word. They all just looked at each other, and then finally one nun spoke.

"It becomes singular," she said.

"Okay, good, and what else does it do?" I asked. "It, well, in a way elevates truth," said a priest.

"Okay, excellent, and what else does it do?" I asked again. People shook their heads.

"Come on," I said, "go for it! What does it do to all other truths?" "It voids them," said Joe.

"Yes, it voids them, and what else happens?" I asked.

"The truth becomes absolute and there can be no other truths," said Mark.

"*Exactamente!*" I said. "And then how do the words 'or' and 'but' back up 'the truth' Eh, what does 'or' do?"

"It gives us choice," said a priest. "Does it really?" I asked.

"It limits us into only two choices in respect to 'the'," said Mark. "*Exactamente!*" I said. "So if I have a third or fourth opinion, I can't voice it because I've been forced into polarity of mind. I either get it or I don't. I agree or I don't. And because you have 'the truth', then I am totally intimidated and so I fold up. And if I don't fold and do speak up, you now use the word 'but' with one 't' and what have you done?"

"I've cancelled out everything you've just said," said Mark.

"Exactly," I said, "and this is why 'the', 'or', and 'but' are by far the ... the most dangerous words in all the world, and have allowed Europe to take over the globe, and it's not because European people are smarter than others! Oh, no, it's that the language they speak gives them a manipulation and arrogance with the one-and-only absolute truth and then nobody else's truths matter. And then hook up 'the truth' to God and/or politics, and you have a culture that respects no other cultures and that's why in México my great-grandfather Leonardis Camargo slaughtered whole Yaqui Indian villages, women and children, too, and he had no regrets, because he had 'the truth' in the name of Jesus Christ."

Tears came to my eyes. "And my great-grandfather wasn't a bad man. He was a good man. It's just that he didn't know any better because language makes us who we are. We talk with language, we think with language, or process all of our feelings through language. So language makes us who we are and our reality what it is. For instance, I now ask you, what happens to the Bible when you take 'the' away and instead put 'a' in front of Bible?"

I stopped and breathed. You could hear a pin drop. "Our Bible becomes one of many," said a priest.

"Yes," I said, "and now there can be many Bibles and many truths. Just breathe. Breathe. And please don't panic. This is good! This is wonderful! Just don't panic, and keep breathing in and breathing out. Good. Good. And now can you begin to see how 'the' has been keeping us in a prison in science, in politics, and not just in religion. Because we're always searching for 'the' answer, 'the' origin of man, 'the' cure for cancer, 'the' cause of this and that, and so we've locked ourselves out of ever gaining understanding, and instead are forever just coming up with new, improved shallow theories and arrogant, self-serving opinions.

"Truly, understand that when your heads hit your pillows tonight, you are going to be Goding. No joke. You will once more have Direct Contact with the Almighty, and this is how Our Six Sister Planets finally started moving out of chaos and violence and being lost and began regaining Harmony and Peace with Creation Creating.

"Like I said, words are manmade and limiting within their own definition and they've only been around 40,000 years at best, and so right now words own us. We don't own them. And this has all been part of our ongoing stages of Godelution, so tonight ask your Guardian Angel, your Genius-Jesusing, for guidance of the Highest Vibrations and you will go on a wonderful adventurous DreamVoyage.

"And also, ask to awake in the morning rested and happy. BIG BIG HAPPY! And Totally at Peace and in Harmony with all the rest of Creation! Ask this, and truly you will RECEIVE, RECEIVE, RECEIVE EVEN FROM THE FURTHEST REACHES OF THE UNIVERSE FOR YOU ARE A HOLLOW BONE! A BUFFALO BONE! AN INSTRUMENT OF GOD-GODING FOR SPREADING HIS/HER *LOVEAMOR* THROUGHOUT ALL THE HEAVENS!"

BOOK THREE

TEN

And that night I went right to sleep and I had one of my old flying dream. Once more I was on a dirt road on Mount Palomar just east of our rancho in Oceanside, California. A whole bunch of happy people were with me and we were spreading out our arms into the wind and laughing and laughing like little kids. Then when a great strong gust of wind came up, our arms turned into wings. Magnificent wings! And now we just took a little short run and leaped off the mountaintop and we were flying and gliding over the great mountainous land of Southern California, going west to the sea. And at the beach, some of us joined in with the seagulls, but like always, I joined in with the pelicans, and now I, too, was gliding along the crest of the waves. Oh, it felt so free and wonderful and easy! BIG BIG EASY! And thusly, I awoke, feeling WONDERFUL!

I started laughing, I felt so good! Then I smelled wild flowers just as I'd smelled in Madrid, Spain when Jesus had come to me, but this time I didn't see Him. Still I said, "Good morning," and heard Jesus say, "Good Morning," back to me.

Then He said, "We're all very proud of you. You're doing very well."

I laughed. "Thanks, but I'll tell you, I was a little unsure a couple of times yesterday."

"So were we," He said, laughing, too. "You? But how can You be unsure?" He laughed all the more.

Then I saw it. "Oh, yeah," I said, "we, Human People, have freewill. I forgot."

And just like that, I couldn't smell the beautiful wild flowers anymore.

I stretched and stretched, and then got up. Oh, I was feeling just fabulous! I went to the bathroom, showered, dressed, and then went out on the balcony to give thanks to the Father Sun, the Right Eye of God, then I went downstairs and I could smell freshly baked rolls and hear laughter before I'd even entered the room where our event was being held. It was Heaven! I could see that as a group, the nuns were bubbling with joy, but a lot of the priests didn't look so good. I guessed that some of them had had a difficult night.

Sister Mary came rushing up and gave me a big hug and kiss each cheek and then so did Sister Margret and two other nuns, but only Father James and Mark came and greeted me. And big burly Joe just watched Mary and Margret hug and kiss me, and he shook his head. I waved for him to come over but he just shook his head again. Myself, I wasn't all that hungry this morning and so all I ate was fruit and cottage cheese, and then I went over to the large expand of windows, said "Hello," to the geese and deer, then turned around to everyone.

"Good morning," I said. "Good morning! Good morning! I hope you all slept very well. Myself, I slept like a baby and had a wonderful flying dream, but," I added, "before we start today, I'd like us to form a circle with chairs so we can all be participants. After all, you are all now Geniuses, and so there are no more leaders for we've all accessed our Kingdom of God that Jesus so wisely told us about. And please bring along your coffee and these delicious wonderful rolls that were freshly baked for us this morning. Mmmmmm, good, eh?"

And so everyone brought up their chair, even a couple of priests who seemed pretty reluctant.

"All right," I said, once were all seated, "so how did you all sleep? Like I said, I slept like a baby and had a wonderful flying dream. So I'd now like you all to share, and please give your name when you do. Okay? So who'd like to start?"

Sister Mary instantly raised her hand with a screech of joy! "So hit it," I said, laughing. "Go for it!"

"Well, my name is Mary, and I'd like to say that usually when I wake up in the middle of the night, I try to go back to sleep, but last night I didn't try to go back to sleep, because I was so excited! So I got up and came down to the kitchen to make myself a cup of coffee and I found Margret and Eve already there and they, too, were so happy and full of energy, but I only visited with them for a little bit, because I just knew that I had to start writing.

"And they were baking anyway, so I didn't feel bad about leaving them in the kitchen and I went into our den, started a fire in the fireplace, and I could barely contain myself, because all these great ideas and insights just kept coming to me. I felt Blessed! I felt like I'd finally really Awakened! And I bet that this is how you felt when you were writing *Rain of Gold*," she added.

I laughed. "Yes, exactly, everyday was Christmas with all these great insights that were being gifted to me every morning from Heaven."

"Yes, this is exactly how I felt this morning," said Mary. "And I hadn't felt like that since I was a very young nun!"

I took in a great big deep breath. "That's wonderful, Mary," I said, "and I'd like you to Know that writing, that keeping a journal, is, in fact, Bibling, and that Bibling is our salvation. Bill, not Shakespeare, but Bill Cartwright my longest best friend who hiked into the Rain of Gold canyon with me that first time and has been a family counselor for over 30 years, he has always told me that the opposite of depression is expression, and when you write down what you're feeling deep inside, you then instantly make room for new possibilities to come into your life. And this is what you were doing, Mary. You giving Birth to God! Because like I said earlier my *mamagrande* always explained to me that we come into this world, into this dimension of reality, pregnant with the Holy Creator, and so this is our Holy Job."

"Then you equate writing a journal to writing the Bible?" asked a priest.

"Sure. What is the Bible? It's a group of stories that connect a tribe to God and Creation, and this is what Mary did last night, and Anne Frank did, and we all do when we get up in the middle of the night and the Stars, our *Familia*, are talking to us. Like Mary said, she felt Blessed. She felt like she'd finally Awakened. And hopefully you'll feel the same thing soon. You see, it took me four months of not talking to get to where Mary got in just one night." I turned back to Mary. "Thank you," I said. "You're on your way, Mary. You are doing your Holy Work here on Mother Earth, which is, of course, to give Birth to God, to give Life to God with All your Life within your very own Kingdom of God that Jesus was sent here to tell us about."

"Yes!" she said. "This is exactly what I was feeling! It's like I Awoke with this great excitement to give Voice, to give Life to all the Goodness that I could feel that I was Receiving in Abundance from the whole Universe! A Hollow Bone I'd become! A Buffalo Bone I'd become! And yet I could never have allowed myself to feel any of this until I understood that Everything is a Verb and that Creation is still going on. It was like my life had reopened in a way I haven't felt since I was a young nun and the bride of my Lord Jesus Christ! Oh, I Awoke with such feeling of ecstasy and warmth and joy and all these feelings and thoughts that, I guess, I'd been holding back for all these years, they now came flooding back to me! Oh, I can hardly wait to go back to sleep tonight, so I can Awake again and continue feeling like I'm once more Directly Receiving from God through his Son Jesus!"

"WONDERFUL!" I said. "WONDERFUL! And so how many of you also Awoke in the middle of the night feeling like this?"

Three more nuns raised their hands, but not one priest.

"I never even got to sleep," said the priest who'd asked if I equated journaling to Bibling. "And what kept me up was, well, why YOU?" He was angry. "Why me?" I said, taking in a deep breath.

"Yes, why you!" he repeated. "I don't see you as being that special, or educated, or anything else!"

"Why me, eh?" I said, closing my eyes so I wouldn't have to keep looking at this priest's angry face, and I could keep focused.

"Well, I'd like you to know that I used to ask myself this same question? I mean, I'd meet people who were slender and all smiles and very spiritual looking and didn't swear, didn't drink *tequila*, didn't look at women and were vegetarian, and they didn't lose their temper, and I say why not them? They're certainly much nicer people than me. But then I remembered that I wasn't a very good wrestler, either, and yet as a freshman I tied the senior who took the California State Championship. And in chess, I beat all the smartest students at school, plus all the faculty, and then it came to me that the real question is not why not them, but why NOT me. Because by asking why not them, I was giving away all of my Powers to them over there and leaving me here, inside, with *nada*, *nada*, nothing. And by asking why not me with All of my Heart and Soul, I was then in a flash bringing in All of the Powers of the Universe into me! And this is what Johann Wolfgang von Goethe wrote about when he so brilliantly said: 'Whatever you can do or dream you can do, begin it! Boldness has genius, power, and magic!'"

"Well, yes," he said, "but—"

I raised up my open hand, palm towards him, closing my eyes, and said in a loud voice, "Please, no 'but' here! Let me finish what I'm saying, because you have asked a very important question! Either we start empowering ourselves, or … or we just keep finger pointing at others, passing judgment, and never take in our full potential, because by you asking this question tells me that you, sir, have over and over chickened out on your OWN POWERS!"

I stopped, opened my eyes, staring at him eye to eye and took in a deep breath. "For instance," I said, "take my last confession back in 1959 when I was 19 years. It's well documented in my book *CrazyLoco Love*."

"You haven't been to confession for 40 years?" he barked at me.

"No, I haven't, and that's not the point!" I barked back. "The point is I started taking my powers back then, and I didn't realize it until later. You see, I did my last confession at the Chapel of the Catholic University of San Diego where I was going to school, and … and it suddenly came to me that yes, I could confess my sins for the Love of God, but not for Fear of God and the pains of hell. And so I said no to that priest, telling him that I would not say that, that I'd rather burn in hell for all eternity than to think for one moment that I was suppose to fear God and believe that … that the Almighty would ever even create such a place as hell.

"I was pumped! I was ready to burn for All Eternity, but I would not back down, and finally the priest was so exasperated at me that he said that if I didn't say that, then I couldn't be a Catholic. This had never entered my mind, but when he said this to me, I then said, "GOOD! GREAT! Then I'm no longer a Catholic!" And I opened up the little curtains of the confessional and stepped out. He got out, too, and started telling me that I just couldn't do that, because I'd been baptized and I'd gone to confirmation and etc. and etc. And I said to him, "Hey, Father, I don't have to listen to anything you tell me anymore, because I'm no longer a Catholic. Goodbye!"

"And I turned and went running and shouting with joy out of the Chapel, and outside I'd never seen the world so beautiful! And that's the night I looked up the word catholic in my Webster Dictionary to find out what I wasn't anymore, and to my shock, I found that it didn't just say universal as we Catholics were always being told, but it also said, 'all-inclusive, of general interest and values and having broad sympathies and understanding; hence, liberal.'

"I screamed with joy, because then I was a real catholic! I REALLY REALLY WAS! And this old priest who'd insisted that I had to have fear of God wasn't a real catholic, because being a catholic meant not just universal, but all-inclusive and having broad understandings and sympathies and so this included me, and so I got in my car and drove over to my cousin's apartment in Ocean Beach where he lived with a bunch of ex-G.I.s, who were also students at the Catholic University, and I told them what had happened and showed them the definition of catholic in my Webster, and instead of rejoicing, they asked me to leave when I wouldn't stop talking so excitedly.

"And those big strong ex-soldiers, who were all older than me, reported me to the priests and the priests informed my parents, but I would not back down, because like I kept telling them, once you get past the Fear of God, then you automatically only see the Absolute Joy and Unconditional Love of God and All, All, All of Creation! The Stars Sing! The Ocean Waves Dance! And the Flowers and Trees smell of Heaven, and for the first time in all my life, I felt Whole and Connected and Happy and FREE!

"So why me? Well, I'll tell you, because I didn't ask why about anyone else and because there are no accidents. Particularly in the Spirit World, and this incident, I'm sure, was what helped prepare me for what Harry Walters and Jack Big Shoulders told me in Nashville, because I was able to grasp what it was that they meant when they told me that they didn't believe in God, that they did God, and they lived with God like my *mamagrande* had lived with *Papito Dios!*

"You see, to go even further, 'belief' is a weak word. You don't 'believe' in your car. You Know your car. And to Know is strong. To 'believe' is weak. It takes us out of the realm of concrete solid knowledge and responsibility, and gives us something to hide behind, because you can't argue with belief, and a person can believe anything they want, and cover up their real agenda. And on the other hand, by doing God by first Walking in Beauty, and then by Harmonizing with All of Creation, then actually Being God-Goding when you find Peace with a capital 'P' within yourself, Totally, Totally makes you Responsible for Everything you Do and you Think. Right Here! Right Now! The buck stops with you!

"Do you see—no, I mean feel what I'm saying? You no longer pass judgment on others. You no longer use the Bible so you can be righteous and full of contempt for others. Eh, are you with me? Like you no longer see handicapped children as even being handicapped. You now see them as Holy Gifts straight from God-Goding that are giving you the opportunity to see the Light of Goding in Everything and Everyone, Equally!" Tears came to my eyes. "You no longer see Down syndrome kids as weird- looking, but as so God-Goding Beautiful with their Big Smiles and Innocent Joy, because you now start doing as the Native Tribes of Central America say when they meet someone, particularly a stranger, 'You are another me, and I am another you,' and you then put your hands behind your back and touch foreheads.

"And homeless people in them I see me and my dad and his poor old Indian mother coming to the Texas border, starving and desperate, and I also remember that my dad went to prison at 13 for stealing six dollars worth of copper ore from the Copper Queen Mining Company of Douglas, Arizona, so he could feed his starving family." Tears were pouring down my face. "So why me, because I asked that question about me, myself, and not you or anyone else and this is what opened up the Flood Gates to All the Powers of the Universe so they could come pouring into me. And I was then able to make a deal with the Almighty to become a writer as great as Homer and/or greater and I didn't even know how to read!

"And why? Because since then I've learned again and again that when we finally see All, All, All People in Ourselves, and especially in the most looked down upon by our society, we then become a VEHICLE OF THE GREATEST ENERGY FORCE AVAILABLE TO US HUMAN BEINGS! Truly, this is why *Of Mice and Men* by John Steinbeck is such a great book! It opens our HeartEyes! And why *The Diary of Anne Frank* is so moving, and *Los de Abajo* by Azuela. So why me? YOU TELL ME! You open up your HeartEyes and see me as you. And special! And wonderful! And as a gift straight from God-Goding! Because this is how I SEE YOU, AND WE ALL, ALL, ALL NEED TO START SEEING EACH OTHER AS, INDEED, ANOTHER US!"

I quit.

I couldn't stop crying, this answer had totally drained me. He looked stunned. He just kept staring at me.

"Look," he finally said. "I'm sorry. I really am. I just thought that you were all about wanting to be an author and famous."

I burst out laughing and laughing. "Oh, my God," I said. "Tell me, have you even read *Rain of Gold*?"

He suddenly looked like a little mouse that'd just been caught in a trap. "I think I better, well, just shut up," he said, glancing around and seeing how everyone was staring at him. "I'm sorry."

"No, please don't be sorry," I said, still laughing and wiping the tears out of my eyes. "It was a question that probably needed to be asked. I'm sure others have been thinking the same thing, but didn't have, well, the guts to ask. Okay, who else?"

Another priest raised his hand. "Go on," I said.

"Matt," he said, "and I, too, didn't sleep the whole night, but what kept coming to me was that you said you didn't sleep for two years. So I finally got dressed and went for a walk, and, well, quite honestly, I began to wonder if you'd been on drugs when you had all of these experiences, because, well," he said, turning red, "I dropped acid when I was a teenager and we went to visit relatives out in Santa Monica, California. And what I experienced frightened me so much that I never took any drugs again, and especially not after one of my cousins in California died from an overdose. So my question to you is this, do you do drugs?"

"Okay," I said, "I'll answer you, but I first need to put this in perspective. As a rule I drink. I don't do drugs, and yet I've taken *peyote* a couple of times in Native American ceremonies with complete supervision and ritual. And I've done mushrooms once in the same way, and I smoke grass now and then with friends."

"How often?"

"Oh, maybe four or five times a year, because what I do on a regular basis is drink. But now," I said, "getting to your real question, was I under the influence when I've had any of my Miraculous Experiences? No, not even a little bit. I was totally clean and sober."

"Okay," he said, "before last night I wouldn't have believed you, but since what happened to me last night, I'm now inclined to believe you, because I swear that the trees began singing to me just as they had when I'd dropped that acid, and then the stars began waltzing, and ... and everything was alive! Totally alive with light and color and so beautiful! And yet I didn't have the fear that I'd had as a teenager. In fact, I felt at peace, and then I began to hear music, a symphony, and I remembered that you said that when God created the Universe He created one verse, one song, and that we all came into manifestation with our own Song, and so I understood that for the first time in my life, that I do have my own Song, and this is what I was hearing and it was making me so happy! Like you say, BIG BIG HAPPY!"

Tears of joy were running down his face, and I went across the room and took Matt in my arms, hugging and kissing him, then I stepped away.

"You, my dear *amigo*," I said, "have just become a Sacred Elder!"

"Me? A Sacred Elder?"

"Yes, you and Mary have Awakened, and become Sacred Elders! Because to be a Sacred Elder is to be in Tune with your own Holy Song that you brought with you from the Heavens along with your Guardian Angel. And so now as Sacred Elders you and Mary need to come out of retirement, and SHOOT INTO INSPIREMENT! For you are now in Harmony with the HOLY MUSIC OF GOD-GODING!"

"You know, maybe you're right," said Matt. "I do feel like this is now a whole new beginning for me."

"It is," I said, with tears of joy streaming down my face, too." I remember what my good friend Louis L'Amour, the western writer, once said to me: "There will come a time when you believe everything is finished, and that will be the beginning." And Mr. L'Amour, who finally even outsold John Steinbeck, KNEW what he was talking about. You, my *amigo*-friend and Mary, *mi amiga*, have AWOKEN! Shooting past all Fear and you are now Ghosting, SongShifting, and Miracle Making just as *Espirito* who followed a deer and her fawn in search of water in the first sentence of *Rain of Gold*.

"And when *Espirito*, meaning Little Spirit, saw the sunlight reflecting off the waterfall in the early morning light, he said, 'A rain of gold!' and thusly it became, and that first sentence used to be 300 words long, but I finally had to just simplify it or I would have lost all my readers, and especially the ones who only spoke

English. "Congratulations! For you two are now Living with one foot on This Side and another foot on the Other Side, and you two are now Living, Breathing *Espiritos* just like that old Indian in *Rain of Gold!* Can you feel it? Is all this finally beginning to make sense to you two? For you two are now Co-Creators with God-Goding, and ready to travel to the Red City of the Americas where All Sacred Elders and Holy *Curanderos* used to travel to before Columbus. And this Red City, some believe was at the great pyramids outside of México City and other scholars are now beginning to think it was the pyramids that are now just being excavated by Guatemala.

"Anyway, Sacred Elders and Holy Healers would come from South America and North America to this Red City and for 10 years they'd exchange Sacred Knowledge and Interplanetary Wisdom with parrots listening, and then they'd go back north and south for 10 years spreading this Sacred Knowledge of Being Interplanetary Miracle Makers. Like creating a rainstorm when a drought came, like healing people by chanting and bringing their Holy Song back into Harmony with the Symphony of God-Goding. Because you see, disease originally meant not-at-ease, and so when a Human is Totally-at-Ease, Totally-in-Tune with their God-Given-Song, then BINGO! All diseases disappear! And so this is now your calling, your Holy Work as Sacred Elders and Holy Healers to help Human People and Our Mother Earth and Father Sky Heal Themselves Spiritually first and then Physically."

Tears of joy were pouring down Matt's face.

"You're right," he said. "You're absolutely right! I was there at that Red City last night and I heard the Symphony of Creation, but still, I'm sure I'll probably go, well, not two years without sleeping like you did, but at least a week—I'M SO EXCITED!"

"Myself," said Mary, "I didn't go to the Red City, but I'm so happy and excited that I'm going to go the rest of my life without sleeping! Oh, this is WONDERFUL! And I can now see that your Great Great Great Great Great Aunt, Mother Of No Specific Child could have easily lived to the age of 165. How could she not when she was Goding!"

All the nuns were up on their feet and cheering, and then congratulating Matt and Mary with hugs and kisses. And big burly Joe was just watching. So I finally walked over and got hold of him, and came pulling him across the room and threw him into the mass of hugging, kissing people.

And there was *Margarita* in the middle of the whole thing, and when she turned and saw big Joe, she opened up her arms to him, but he was so shocked that at first he didn't know what to do. But then this face burst into a huge smile, and he went for it, hugging this woman that he'd been in love with for over 60 years!

ELEVEN

We took a break. I went to my room, put on my running shoes, and then took off running around the lake. I'd been running for nearly 40 years, ever since I'd taken up wrestling in high school and I usually ran about 20 to 25 miles a week. Four runs of about three to four miles, then one day a week I'd go a 10 mile distance, and on these runs, I'd do the first mile at about an eight minute pace, then I'd drop down to a seven minute pace, and at this faster speed I'd no longer be jogging but running, and it would be easier on my knees because I'd be using the front part of my feet more, and pushing off with my toes and so it felt like sailing!

Oh, I loved running! It was a natural high! And also, right now, I'd get to be alone, so I could let things kind of catch up with me, because oh, boy, had we just covered a lot of ground. Never in a million years did I ever dream that these old farts—I mean these old nuns and priest would be so Alive and Open and Available!

But then up ahead, who did I see, it was Mark and he was running, too, and really kicking ass. And normally I would've pushed myself dropping to an under 6 minute pace to catch the person and/or people ahead of me, but I didn't. I stayed well behind and just followed Mark as he went on trails through the woods and alongside creeks and it was wonderful. Once we jumped a herd of deer, and we came back laughing, but never having said a word until we'd returned. I was the first to speak.

"So how did it go for you last night, Mark?" I asked.

He took in a deep breath. "Very productive," he said, "and yet very strange, but I'd like to save my comments for the group," he added.

"Okay," I said, and we parted and I went up to my room, took a quick shower, and then went back downstairs.

Instantly, I could feel the difference. The whole room felt in Harmony and Alive and Full of Love*Amor*! Even the priests as a group, now seemed happy and relaxed. People were talking excitedly and laughing and having a very good time!

I got myself a cup of hot water and brought out my lavender Yogi Licorice tea bag. I sat down in our circle of chairs and began dunking my tea bag up and down in the hot water until it was a golden color. I never drank coffee or caffeinated tea. I was always already so naturally high that if I felt any better I'd probably get arrested. Seeing me sit down, the others began taking their seats, too.

"Okay," I said, once everyone was seated, "as you can all see we've become a pretty relaxed happy group."

A priest raised his hand. "Okay," I said. "Go on."

"Have you ever read the book *The Outsider* by Colin Wilson?" he asked. I shook my head.

"I think you should," he said. "Because what Wilson does, is that he gives us understanding of the human mind and shows us how the human mind can only handle so much before it, well, cracks, or goes insane. And he uses the examples of Van Gogh, Vaslav Nijinsky, Lawrence, Rimbaud, T.S. Eliot, all these gifted heavyweights of the arts, and so not only did I have trouble sleeping last night, but I ended up throwing up my whole dinner." Tears were streaming down his face "And what kept coming to me, from deep inside of me, was, well, if we do, in fact, take 'the' away from the Bible, then does this mean that you're suggesting that we take 'the' away from what Jesus Christ told us about Him being 'the' only way?"

I took in a deep breath and closed my eyes, asking for guidance. This was a big one. Maybe even the biggest one, because this one hit the nail right on the head of our entire Western Civilization. I took in more deep breaths and suddenly I smelled wild flowers, and so I once more Knew that Our Lord Jesus was here with us. I opened my eyes, and no, I couldn't see Jesus, but I could sure feel His Full Powers of Love*Amor* nothing but Love*Amor* and His Sacred Energy was going up and down my spine with a Tingling Sensations that got so hot that I began sweating.

"Well," I said, turning to this priest. "I can well understand why this would be a pretty disturbing thought, because I, too, got pretty upset when this notion first came to me. But then I prayed and asked for guidance, turning it all over to God."

"BUT!" he yelled. "How can I now turn it all over to God through His Only Son Jesus, if we take 'the' away?"

I closed my eyes and took in a deep breath, smelling the Wild Flowers, and then another deep breath, smelling these most wonderful smelling Wild Flowers again, and I now opened my eyes, feeling Totally Connected.

"Excuse me," I said, "but with whom am I speaking?"

"Oh, Adam," he said. "Sorry. I forgot. I haven't been thinking very clearly." "Well, Adam," I said, getting out of my chair and moving back by the large expanse of windows, so I wouldn't be affected by his energy, "you know, I'm being told right now... that what you need to do is to find this answer on your own. Because, for me, to tell you my answer wouldn't be a good fit, and this is a big one. Maybe even 'the' biggest for most Christians."

"All right, but how do I do this?" he asked once again. "Last night, I swear, I felt so confused and upset that it was even difficult for me to pray. I kept losing focus, because so much of what you've shared with us seems true, and even feels true, and also, I read your whole book more than once, and so ... well, I just don't know what to do, because I'm afraid that if I lose my Church and the whole structure that I've been brought up with, I might lose God and end up cutting off not just one ear, BUT BOTH EARS!"

He stopped and took in several deep breaths, and blew out fast each time. "I now realize why there was a very large part of me that was against having you come to see us. We're old! We're retired! And so we just want to make peace within us, so we can—"

He was trembling, and tears were pouring down his face, but he wasn't bothering to wipe them off. I walked over to him and took the white handkerchief out of my back pocket that I always carried that my mother had given me years ago and had little red flowers and green leaves that she'd embroidered on it.

"Here," I said, "from my mother to you."

"Thank you," he said, taking the white handkerchief and wiping his eyes. "No, thank you," I said. "For Totally Opening your Whole Heart and Soul." He laughed. "Trust me, I didn't mean to," he said. "It just all came out."

"Yes, and that's the way it normally is in giving and in receiving. For this is who we, Human Beings, really are, Holy Instruments of God."

"There!" he shouted. "YOU'VE DONE IT AGAIN! And this is awful, because I really did love *Rain of Gold* and I really do love all that you've told us, but it also, well, destroys the Church! MY CHURCH! THE WHOLE WORLD'S CHURCH! Just look what all this profound thinking has done to you! You're not even Catholic anymore!"

The whole room was silent. Adam had certainly brought everything back to square one. Then *Margarita* spoke with such a gentle tone that it helped us all to regain composure.

"Does it really destroy the Church?" she asked. "Or does it help Our Beloved Church to become what it originally professed to be, universal and all-inclusive."

"BUT THAT'S NOT WHAT JESUS OR THE BIBLE SAY!" shouted Adam.

"Excuse me," I said, "but you do know that most scholars now agree that Jesus spoke Aramaic when he was with us here on earth." "Yes, I understand that," said Adam.

"Well," I said, "there is no word 'the' in the Aramaic Language." "What? What are you saying?"

"I'm saying," I said, "that Jesus never said that He was 'the' only way. The Greek's translation added 'the' and 'only' was added by the English. So Our Lord Jesus said that He was 'a way', and/or He simply said He was 'way', and so His message was Totally about Inclusion and He was inviting All of Us to Be Sons and Daughters of God, Equally. Even the Romans and not just the Jews. And this only makes sense, because the Roman Empire controlled the whole known world and Jesus, Son of God, wanted to bring Peace to the Whole World just as He wants to do today."

Adam bent over, gripping his stomach. "Then you're really serious about all this you've shared with us, even about the Vatican mo – mo!" He began gagging, but nothing was coming up.

Mark and *Margarita* rushed to help Adam over to a couch to lie down, and his body continued trembling and jerking.

"Okay," I said, "is anyone else feeling kind of sick." Half a dozen hands went up.

"You know," said another priest, "if we'd been told all this as young seminarians I'm quite sure we wouldn't have had any trouble accepting all this, because it does make sense. Why would the Son of God not invite us all to become sons and daughters of the Holy Creator equally? And I can also see how this could revolutionize the whole Church and help unite all the different religions of the world. So yes, I can see all this in my mind. I really can. But here, in my gut, I'm too old to accept any of this. I agree with Adam. You've come to us 50 to 60 years too late and what we now want is peace and tranquility."

"And you are who?" I asked.

"Oh, excuse me, Michael," he said.

"And how old are you, Michael?" I asked. "I'm 80," he said.

"Look," I said, "you're only 80. You've only been into the most perfect age of 78 for two little years, so come on, stop bullshitting yourself and realize that you're just getting started and you have a RESPONSIBILITY OF BECOMING A SACRED ELDER!" I shouted, startling the shit out of him.

"But look what just happened to Adam," he said sheepishly, "and to Van Gogh. There's only so much that the human mind can take."

"You're right," I said. "There is only so much that the human mind can take. But you now Know that we don't just process information with our mind and 4 senses. You now Know that we have

3 centers for processing information, and with our Full Natural 13 Senses, then there are no limitations. Van Gogh, Nijinsky, Rimbaud, all of these guys would have had no *problemas* if their Full Natural 13 Senses had been firing."

"Really, you think so?"

"I KNOW SO!" I yelled. "And you Know it was a capital 'K', too! Look, Western Civilization is like a big 12 cylinder engine that's only using 4 of its cylinders, so, of course, it's easy to go berserk. And also note, all those who broke down were men, not women, and Anne Frank and my two *mamagrandes* endured 10,000 times more horror and confusion and still they didn't go insane, but instead THESE WOMEN ROSE UP WITH THEIR FULL POWERS AS ANGELS STRAIGHT FROM GOD!

"So no! You will not check out! You are 80 years and Totally, Totally Available! So stand up! Come on, get your ass out of that chair, and LEAP into your Balanced Female and Male Energies and take on your RESPONSIBILITY of becoming a Sacred ELDER! There's no turning back for you guys! You took an oath to Be Of Service for God-Goding, and so you now keep your word, because you see, the aging process from a Spiritual Point of View starts reversing when you reach the age of 65 and you have Balanced your Male and Female Energies! And so you are 65 going on 55, and then 75 going on 60, then 80 going on 65, then 104 going on 78, because Spirit Aging can actually override physical aging to the degree that you accept your Full God-Given Spirituality. Tell him, Mary! Tell him, Matt! Tell Michael about all this Fantastic Great Youthful Energy that came BURSTING into you two last night!"

And so Mary told him that she was 86 and she, too, had thought she was over the hill, that her days of service were over, but then last night all these great feelings of Love*Amor* had come BURSTING into her Heart and Soul, and she now felt as Full of Energy and Purposeful as when she'd been a young nun.

"And I can now see," she said to Michael, "that I'd lost faith, well, not in God, but in my ability to make any difference, because of all the undermining politics of clerical life and all the terrible news that we see on T.V."

"Exactly," said Matt, "but now with the Vatican moving to Ireland for 100 years, and then to México where my grandparents were from for another 100 years, has sent my whole world into such a spin of WONDERMENT AND POSSIBILITIES, that if I just keep calm and don't let myself go into fear or doubt, then I'm flying in ECSTASY WITH SUCH ENERGY that I, too, now feel like a young bride of Our Lord Jesus! And also remember, the Vatican was moved to France for nearly a century," he added. "So there has been a precedent."

"No, that's not true," said Michael. "What happened was that the King of France appointed his own Pope. And what Mr. Villaseñor is suggesting is that the Vatican itself will move to Ireland. Is this correct?" he said, turning to me.

I nodded. "Yes, this was part of the information that was Transmitted into me in Madrid."

"When Jesus came to you?" said Michael with a tone of sarcasm. "Yes," I said, refusing to be taken in by his energy.

"And it makes SO MUCH SENSE!" shouted Matt excitedly. "Because back then our whole known world was centered around the Mediterranean Sea, and so Italy, Rome, seemed the logical location to place the head of the Catholic Church, but now with what we know of the entire globe, it only makes sense to move the Vatican, and keep moving it, the head of the Catholic Church, every 100 years around the globe! OH, THIS IS SO EXCITING! And it makes so much sense! I CAN ACTUALLY SEE IT ALREADY DONE!"

"YES!" I said. "Because it's already WRITTEN IN THE STARS! You see, the Future doesn't necessarily come after the Present! Time is circular! This movement is, in fact, already completed, finished, done, and a long forgotten memory in the furthest reaches of the UNIVERSE!"

"HE'S RIGHT!" shouted Matt. "And Our Lord Jesus is with us RIGHT HERE! RIGHT NOW! He's never left us! Oh, I can now SEE IT ALL SO CLEARLY! This is WONDERFUL! And Gaelic makes perfect sense! And then in México an Indian dialect of the Yucatan! Yes, the language of your Great Great Great Great Aunt Mother Of No Specific Child! And in doing all this, Our Holy Catholic Church becomes of Goding. Not of men. But of men and of women with us having Women Popes and Women Cardinals and Women Bishops and Women Priests, and ... and can't you all see it? Our Church becomes SACRED AND FOREVER CHANGING and ... and will then continue for 50,000 years? Could this be right?" he asked.

"It's perfectly right," I said, "because Our Mother Earth works in 26,000 year cycles. One cycle being of male energy like we're just completing, and the other being of female energy that we are just starting. And so 52,000 years is one complete cycle of male and female energy, and by lasting for 50,000 more years, Our Holy Church will then be in the Sacred Flow of Creation Creating, and hence, Eternal! And this is exactly what Jesus Transmitted into me in Madrid, Spain back in November of 1992 when *mi familia* and I and a group of Native Americans went to Spain to forgive the king and queen for all of the atrocities that Spain committed around the globe, and plant our Snow Goose Global Thanksgiving Flag from World-Wide Harmony and Peace and ... and Abundance for All!

"But then I lost focus. My thinking head had taken over, and so I was full of doubt and fear and ... and feeling ridiculous. Who was I to think that I could come with a group of people to forgive a king and queen? So feeling exhausted and full of confusion I lied down in my little hotel room bed and asked God for help, and, well, I must've fallen asleep because when I awoke, I could see that there was a man at the far end of my little room and he was surrounded by a Bright Golden Light that lit up the whole room and yet was soft and didn't hurt my eyes.

"I rubbed my eyes and looked again. This is all well documented in the book *Beyond Rain of Gold* I'm presently writing, and suddenly I Knew with a capital 'K' that this was Jesus, and so I got up on my elbows to see Him better and I could see that He was hovering about two feet off the floor. I got up and went to

Him and this was when He reached into His chest and brought out His Most Holy Sacred Heart. A real pulsating heart with arteries and everything and He reached out handing me His Heart*Corazon*, and...and in the act of doing this, I understood that He was endorsing our trip to Spain and everything that we were prepared to do, and then Miraculously He, who'd been of brown skin and looking part American Indian like me, now changed into all the different Human People of the world. In features! In skin color! In robes! In eyes! In everything! And this was when I Knew that Jesus is in Everyone of Us. You, Me, We, ALL OF US! And I was no longer lost and I once more KNEW EXACTLY, EXACTLY why we'd come to Spain and what we were to do!"

"So what did you do?" asked another priest. "Did you actually meet with the king and queen and forgive them and Spain?"

"No, not quite, but look, like I said, it's all well documented in *Beyond Rain of Gold*, and...and I'm wiped out right now," I added, gripping my forehead. "I need to lie down, and/or have a beer and a *tequila*. Wow! Let's just call it a day, and we'll get into all this *mañana*. Because, remember, tomorrow is *otro milagro de Dios!*"

Mark raised his hand. "Excuse me," he said, looking at me, "but when we got back from running you asked me how it went for me last night. And I told you very productive, and yet very strange, and that I didn't want to say anything to you about it, because I wanted to share it with our group."

I nodded. "Okay, so please do share."

He stood up. "You see," he said, turning to everyone, "I'm not here because I had a nervous breakdown as some of you might believe. I'm here, because, well, I, too, proposed to a nun and she accepted." He stopped, taking in a deep breath. "So we are now both leaving the Church so we can marry. And I'll tell you," he said, "I'm so much in love with *Josefina*, whom I met in Ecuador, that my whole world has literally changed upside down, and I've come to the realization that Our Lord God can be nothing but Love*Amor*, and that all there is, IS LOVE*AMOR* THROUGHOUT THE UNIVERSE!"

He stopped again, breathing deeply. "You see," he added, "I'd never heard of Mr. Villaseñor or of his writings, but then I was sent here for six months so I can, well, reconsider what *Josefina* and I are proposing to do, and I found that our nuns here were talking about nothing else but *Rain of Gold*, so I read the book not once, but five times so far, and I now see that what I saw in our Native American Sisters of Ecuador is what *Rain of Gold* is really all about. Just like his two beloved grandmothers, *Doña Guadalupe* and *Doña Margarita*, didn't 'believe' in God but 'Lived' with God and were so full of Wisdom and Pure *Amor* and an Indestructible Faith in the Almighty, so are our Sisters in Ecuador.

"And it troubled me, because our American and European Sisters are good- hearted wonderful people, too, and yet I could feel that something was missing, but I had no idea what that something was until now that Mr. Villaseñor, himself, told us that even he, who wrote *Rain of Gold*, didn't understand his own book until that Navajo and big Lakota explained his own book to him. Then I understood that language truly does own us, as Mr. Villaseñor has stated.

"Also it makes sense to me that we have more than 5 senses. For instance, when I was about 10 years old, my younger brother Luke suddenly awoke in the middle of the night and started telling us that our dad had had a car accident and that he was dying, and so we had to pray, so he wouldn't die. My mother and I and my sisters and little brother all started praying, and we received a call about an hour later that our dad had been in a terrible wreck, and yet miraculously he was going live.

"And so, what I'm saying with all this is … that with our Natural Multi-Sensory Perception of our Full 13 Senses and our understanding that Creation is still going on at this very moment, then that experience my younger brother had becomes available to all of us. And this is Our Future. Our Destiny. For the Miraculous to become part of Our Norm. Tell me, how else can we expect to keep going if we don't move into a Reality of Miracles!"

He glanced around.

"There is no other way," he continued. "Because it's going to take Miracles to get us out of our present situation, and now that we know that we have 3 Centers for processing experience and information we can do it. We really can, especially now that we know that our Thinking Brain Center is our smallest computer, and that Our Intuitive Heart Center and Our Psychic Soul Center are LIMITLESS! Just imagine if all of our Catholic schools began teaching that we have a Multi-Sensory Perception of 13 Senses! Our youth would start Genius-Jesusing!"

He couldn't stop smiling. "What a concept Jesus-Geniusing! What Possibilities! What Energy! What Purity! What—oh, my God-Goding! This is all so wonderful! It's like ALL, ALL, ALL OF ME HAS BECOME ALIVE AND I'M NOW NO LONGER 'WITH' JESUS. I am 'of' Jesus, meaning that I, too, am now a Son of God!"

Smiling, he glanced around once more. "And now that I can see that this is the something that was missing with our American and European Sisters and Priests; the understanding that we have 13 Natural Senses, that Creation is ongoing and so we are in Active Partnership with God, then I, too, like Mr. Villaseñor's grandmothers, are FULL OF HOPE AND INDESTRUCTIBLE FAITH because I no longer 'believe' in Miracles! Oh, no, I 'KNOW' Miracles and so I can now 'DO' Miracles just as my younger brother Luke did at such a tender age!"

He stopped and took in a great big deep breath.

"Oh, for the first time in my life I feel Complete and Whole," he said, "and I'm so happy! BIG BIG HAPPY! Being not 'WITH' Jesus, but Being 'OF' Jesus and remembering that Jesus told us that what He did, we would do more, and we can! WE REALLY CAN DO MORE!"

Father James stood up and began applauding. Instantly everyone joined him, standing up and applauding, too.

I was crying.

I was crying with tears of ecstasy streaming down my face, and then the scent of Wild Flowers came to me. I smiled, and said, "Thank You, Jesus!"

"Thank you," I heard Him say right back to me.

I wiped the tears out of my eyes with the back of my right hand, glanced around, and I could see that people were Aglow with Golden Light.

"WE'RE ON OUR WAY!" I shouted.

"Yes, we are!" said Mark. "And I can also see that—as we Catholics come out of hiding behind archaic dogma and take on what it means to Be A Complete And Real Catholic with the whole definition of all-inclusive, of general interest and value, having broad sympathies and understanding, hence liberal, that this will move Us into the Holy Light of God-Goding by accepting what Albert Einstein proved, that all there is, is change, and Creation never stopped and never began, and is ongoing Right Here! Right Now! Forever Within Creation Creating! And this isn't just a wild dream, but OUR RESPONSIBILITY—not just as Catholics but as Human Beings—AND TRUE FOLLOWERS OF JESUS CHRIST! To do as Our Lord did on the cross and show Compassion, Forgiveness, Kindness, and drop all of our archaic dogma of judgment and righteousness and exclusion!

"And we do this—as I learned in Ecuador and Mr. Villaseñor shared with us—by doing as some tribes do in Central America. When walking through the rainforest and two strangers meet, they automatically drop their weapons, place both of their hands behind their back, touch foreheads, and say, 'You are another me, and I am another you,' and they then look into each other's eyes and smile. And this morning I did this with myself in the mirror, and I saw—"

"AND YOU SAW AN ANGEL!" shouted Mary.

"That's right!" said Mark. "I saw an Angel and realized for the first time in my life that that's who we all really are ... Angels, Messengers of Light, as Albert Einstein said he was when he received his Theory of Relativity."

"The same thing happened to me!" said Mary. "And I wasn't going to share this, because I was so embarrassed, but now I'm not, because I can now see that this is our true responsibility as Followers of Jesus to see that we are all Angels!"

With great excitement people now began talking among themselves. Father James winked at me and I nodded to him, then big, burly Joe came forward.

"Well, I didn't see an Angel in my mirror this morning," said Joe, "but I did see a very happy face!"

Everyone laughed.

And it was *Margarita* who now also spoke up. "I also didn't see an Angel in my mirror," she said. "But I, too, saw a very happy face."

And saying this, she began walking across the room to Joe with such regal confidence. Joe was all eyes, taking in her beauty, and maybe they didn't see it yet, but I'm sure that most of us did see it. *Margarita* and Joe were, indeed, Aglow with Angelic Love*Amor* Energy as they drew closer and closer to each other.

Then *Margarita* placed both of her hands behind herself and bent forward. Joe placed his two hands behind himself, bending forward, and they touched foreheads, oh, so gently. Then they straightened up, and looked into each other's eyes. No happier smiles had ever been seen on this side of Heaven. Before our very eyes, Joe and *Margarita* had TRANSFORMED! Not only becoming Angels of Illuminating Light, but actually getting younger and younger and younger!

Then it was *Margarita* who reached out to take the large man in her arms. And Joe wasn't shocked this time and took her in his arms, too. There wasn't a dry eye in the whole room. *Margarita* 91. Joe 86. And they'd known each other for over 60 years and now, at last, they were in each other's arms, and ... and kissing.

"Well, well," said Mark, "I almost wasn't going to share any of this, but look at the results it has caused. So are you two," he continued, "going to join *Josefina* and me and also get married? Remember, this is a very emotionally-driven planet, so any time we bring Love*Amor* to Mother Earth we help heal her."

"Well, then if that's the case," said Joe, turning to *Margarita*, "then I say—"

"YES!" shouted the ex-mother superior. "We certainly want to do our share of helping to Heal Our Beloved Mother Earth!"

"Sounds good to me," said Joe, never letting go of her.

"Oh, I remember the first time I saw you, Joe," she said. "You were clearing land of rock and brush in preparation for a garden behind our convent. It was a hot summer day and you took off your shirt and, well, you looked like a Greek god. I couldn't stop staring at you, so I ran and would never let myself ever look at you again, even when you were fully clothed."

His eyes got huge. "And all these years I thought that I'd done something or said something that had offended you."

"Oh, no!" she said. "All these years I've been afraid of these feelings I've had for you, Joe!"

"And ... and I've been afraid of these feelings I've had for you," he said.

You could hear a pin drop. Two Hearts, two Souls, finally coming together after all these years.

I took in a deep breath, instantly smelling Wildflowers again. I glanced around, and here was Our Lord Jesus by the windows at the far end of the room. He was smiling. I smiled, too, and then in a quick flash, Jesus came spinning all through us in a Wild Flower Scent of Holy Light!

"Well," said Mark, glowing with Jesus's Light, "I can now see that it was no accident that I was sent to Ecuador and fell in love. And it's no accident I was sent here for the 6 months and introduced to *Rain of Gold*. And it's no accident that your brilliant good Sisters had Mr. Villaseñor come to us. For everything that he has shared with us; we, all of us, already Knew deep inside our Kingdom of God, which we have finally activated, and we now understand that Creation is still happening and there's nothing but Love*Amor* throughout the Whole Universe, and we are all 'of' Jesus and so we, too, are Sons and Daughters of God.

"And to move our Holy Church to Ireland makes total sense. And not because I'm part Irish, but because, remember, Ireland saved Western Civilization by keeping all the records and books through the Dark Ages, and then what did the English do? Starve us! Enslave us through indentured servitude! So, yes, Ireland, then México, who's suffered even more, then the Philippines, of course, and the Purity of Love*Amor* for God-Goding, a Verb, will be re-established, and these last 2,000 years will then be nothing compared to our Grand Fabulous All-Inclusive Future of Our Holy Church! And then *Josefina* and I can be married and we don't have to leave the Church, and Joe, you and *Margarita* can do the same!

"OH, I AWOKE LAUGHING THIS MORNING, I felt so happy with all that Mr. Villaseñor has been sharing with us!" shouted Mark. "And then I looked in the mirror and saw that I'd given Birth to God by... by becoming my very own Guardian Angel, and so yes, of course, it's true that I, that we all come across the Universe gathering Stardust to help God-Goding plant His Ongoing Garden of Heaven on Earth! And so I say, 'THANK YOU, GOD-GODING! Thank You for orchestrating this Whole Living, Breathing Symphony of Creating Creation! WE ARE BLESSED!"

And having said all this, Mark just stood before us SMILING AND GLOWING WITH ECSTASY! And his VIBRATIONAL FREQUENCIES were of such Intensity that they didn't just affect us, who were in the room with him, but they affected all of Creation Creating around Our Whole Mother Earth, AND TO THE FURTHEST REACHES OF OUR UNIVERSE!

Outside the Canadian Geese began HONKING with *gusto,* and coming up to the windows, flapping their GREAT GIGANTIC WINGS!

And the Trees took on a Happy Breeze and began dancing their limbs!

And the Grass and Flowers took on JESUS'S HOLY SCENT OF HEAVEN ON EARTH!

Oh, yes, Our Beloved Mother Earth certainly is OUR MOST EMOTIONALLY LOVE*AMOR* DRIVEN PLANET OF OUR SIX SISTER PLANETS! And so healing her, we help heal HER BELOVED TWIN SISTER, too!

TWELVE

Time stood still.

And more Holy Timeless Time stood still. It was like we, too, were all in a trance within our own delicious-smelling Kingdom of God, feeling a smooth relaxing Happy Holy Silence. Then it was finally Father James who was the first to speak.

"Well," he said, "to help all the rest of us become our own Guardian Angel, I suggest that this is a good time for us to bring out that special bottle of *tequila* that we purchased in your name, Victor. Eh, what do you all say? Should we go over what we've learned before we break for dinner, or should we have a shot of *tequila?*"

"*TEQUILA!*" shouted everyone.

"Good, then *tequila* it is!" said Father James. "And we had difficulty finding it, Victor," he added, turning to me, "but we were finally able to locate a few bottles of your favorite."

"*Herradura?*" I said, licking my lips.

"Yes!"

"Oh, wonderful!" I said. "So then, by all means, let's have a shot right now!" We all went into the big main dining room with the large stone fireplace and Mary brought out a tray of those tiny beautiful wine glasses that people normally use after dinner for sherry or port. We were each served a generous shot of *tequila,* then we gathered in front of the fireplace, which had a good-size fire going.

"TO OUR SISTERS, who had the courage to invite the author of *Rain of Gold* to come to see us!" said Father James.

"And to Victor who also had the courage to accept our invitation!" added Mary.

We all lifted our beautiful little crystal glasses and took a sip of our *Herradura*, which originally had been made by Villaseñors.

"And now I'd like to make a toast to Our First Lady Pope!" I added.

"TO OUR FIRST LADY POPE!" people shouted, and most of us shot down our remaining *tequila*.

"OH, THAT FEELS SO GOOD!" yelled Sister Mary. "The burn of *tequila* and the image of Our First Lady Pope being guided by Our Blessed Mother and Jesus and Legions of Angels to Ireland!"

And saying this, Mary gave a shout of joy, then suddenly threw her glass into the fire where it shattered against the stone.

We were all SHOCKED!

But no one more than Sister Mary herself.

But then she started giggling and laughing with such wild abandonment that two other nuns followed her example, finishing off their *tequilas* and throwing their own glasses into the fire, too, and now all three nuns were beside themselves, laughing with *carcajadas*!

The priests, I could see, were stunned. But not the nuns. Oh, no, now it became a major event of more nuns finishing off their *tequilas* and throwing their glasses into the fire, then laughing with wild crazy*loco gusto*!

"Well, well," said Father James, serving Mark and me and himself another *tequila*, "I can now see why Native Americans call liquor fire water. Our good nuns are, indeed, on fire!"

"Amen!" said Mark.

"Awomen! Achildren! Amen!" I added as we now sipped our second shots. "My dad, a bootlegger, always told us that in the first half of a liquor bottle you find God, but in the second half you find the Devil if... if you're not careful."

They both laughed and Matt now came over to join us along with two other priests. James was serving them their second shot when we saw that our good nuns were not going to let us, the men, out-do them. Oh, no, a couple of giggling full-of-mischief sisters had brought out another tray of crystal glasses and Mary now opened up another bottle of *Herradura* and began serving.

"FANTASTIC!" said Mark. "Just look at them and hear their laughter! It was also *Josefina's* great joyful laugh that OPENED MY SOUL AND GAVE WINGS TO MY *CORAZÓN*!!"

"There's no turning back for them now!" said Matt.

"Yes, and it's about time!" I added.

"I agree," said Father James, "and in support, I'm joining them!"

And saying this, this most dignified looking of all priests, who was, in fact, an Archangel, now walked across the room, drank off his *tequila*, then with a shout of *gusto* he, too, threw his antique French crystal glass into the fire where it also shattered against the stone.

"TO OUR FIRST LADY POPE!" he shouted.

"YES!" screeched the nuns. "TO OUR FIRST LADY POPE!"

"May she be full of LOVE AND COMPASSION!" yelled one nun.

"MAY SHE BE AS STRONG AND CUNNING AS VICTOR'S FANTASTIC GRANDMOTHERS!" shouted Mary.

"AMEN! AWOMEN! ACHILDREN!" shouted several nuns.

"AWOMEN! ACHILDREN! AMEN!" shouted Matt and Mark.

"EXACTLY!" I said. "Snow Geese flying in V-Formations across the Father Sky with mother and children leading and men following in front!"

And so we continued celebrating, but, I can tell you, that not all the priests were happy with what was going on. Finally one priest stepped forward.

"This is PRECISELY why so many of us priests were against bringing this author of *Rain of Gold* to see us! Look what has happened to us! These glasses are genuine antique French crystal, and you're behaving as disrespectful as when the author's grandmother would pray her rosary in the outhouse!"

I was impressed. This tall elegant-looking priest had never uttered a single word until now that he was livid with rage. And I was just about to go over to him and offer him a double *tequila* when our feisty little Sister Mary came forward, getting right into his face.

"OH, STOP IT, JOHN!" she barked. "We're the ones who wash and care for these glasses! NOT YOU! So don't now start acting as if these French crystal glasses are so important to you! What's really bothering you? Eh, John, could it be our exuberance, and that maybe we won't do your laundry anymore!?"

And saying this, Mary BURST OUT LAUGHING LIKE THERE WAS NO TOMORROW! And the nuns followed her, laughing their heads off! The tall priest looked mortified.

"OH, JOHN, JUST LOOK AT YOU!" shouted Mary. "You, who's always so full of yourself and can never stop lecturing us, now doesn't know what to say! THIS IS WONDERFUL! Here, let me hug you and give you a kiss, my frightened little boy!"

But John wouldn't let Mary get near him.

"Excuse me," said *Margarita*. People quickly quieted down. "Because, you see, even though I haven't thrown my glass into the fire and am going to keep this little glass to remind me of this day for the rest of my life—I do accept Sister Mary's behavior."

She stopped and coughed, clearing her throat and she now took on the full power of her well-practiced air of a Mother Superior before continuing.

"You see, we must begin to understand what it means to relocate our Vatican from Rome to Ireland. This is going to be nothing less than as large a global statement as when our 13 little colonies broke away from the eminent powers of Great Britain. It was the fall of royalty. It was the rise of everyday people. For the people, of the people, and by the people, and this time we women, along with the help of priests like Father James and Mark and Matt, will be an equal part of the people, by the people, for the people, as we move to Ireland and … and not just have Our First Woman Pope, but also move away from the extravagance of French crystal to goblets in Ireland, then *copitas de varro* in Mexico."

"*Copitas* of what?" said Father John.

"BRILLIANT!" shouted Mark, putting two fingers to his mouth and whistling an ear-piercing whistle. "You are ABSOLUTELY right, *Hermana Margarita!* Cups made of clay that are affordable by everyone! Instead of French crystal that's only affordable by the very rich! Oh, yes, I can see it now, our move to Ireland will include bringing a halt to these last 2,000 years of excess and corruption and bring us back to the reality that Our Lord Jesus was born in a manger, and so the Foundation of Our Church has always been about Humility, Kindness, and Forgiveness; in other words, not just supporting the poor like Mother Teresa so well did, but for us to walk our talk, embracing the purity that less is more, and Create a World of Inclusion where it's easier to be Good-Hearted People!

"Truly, after working with the poverty of Ecuador, it was an embarrassment for me to see all the wealth that our church has accumulated over the centuries and how some of my fellow priests would brag about how much money they'd brought to their diocese as if they were working on Wall Street. Is this what God had in mind when He sent His Son to us? COME ON! LET'S GET REAL!"

"Are you then suggesting that we abandon, or worse, destroy the Vatican in Rome?" asked John.

"Of course not," said *Margarita*, stepping in. "That great ostentatious place will be made into a museum of some sort and opened to the public!"

"I agree," I said, closing my eyes. "The walls will come down, and it will become a great museum and a great concert hall, and all the gold, that was globally stolen from the Heart*Corazon* of Our Beloved Mother Earth, will be given back through education over a 400-year plan, and...and the Queen of Spain will once more lead, just as she did 500 years ago with Columbus. You see," I said, opening my eyes, "it's always really been about Music, our 8th Sense, that activates our 3rd Center, Our Soul Computer FOR THE GREATER GLORY OF GOD!

"So, yes, the Vatican in Rome will continue to lead by 'following in front', but no longer with dogma and ... and instead through Our Sacred Symphony of Creation Creating, which is the Holy Voice of God-Goding, and as our locations of the Vatican move around the globe for the next 50,000 years so will the Music of Our Beloved Church keep Changing and Growing and Glowing with ... with Compassion, meaning passion in common and Love*Amor* for there's only One Race, the Human Race, and we are All, All, All Equally Children Of God!"

I stopped, took in a deep breath, held, then blew out fast.

"Oh, I'll never forget the first time I heard Enya. I just knew that through this Incredible Instrument of Pure Heartfelt Music, God was calling, calling, and informing us all about Our First Lady Pope and Our Godelution Movement of Our Church to Ireland.

"Truly, next time you listen to Enya close your eyes, place both hands over your Heart and your Soul will come Alive, and you will Know that it's all about HARMONIZING OUR SPIRITUAL VIBRATIONAL FREQUENCIES WITH THE SYMPHONY OF OUR UNIVERSE!"

"ONE UNITED VERSE! ONE UNITED SONG!" shouted Mary, finishing off her second *tequila* with *gusto!*

"Yes, thank you, Mary," I said. "And this is exactly why Jesus came to me in Madrid, Spain, because, you see, it's never been about great cathedrals and accumulating gold—which automatically leads to corruption. No, it's always been like what Jesus did for me. For each of us to ... to reach into our own chest and give each other the most precious treasure we have to give and ... and that's OUR PULSATING HEART*CORAZÓN!*"

"Yes, the dropping of our doubts and fears and weapons and putting our hands behind our backs and touching foreheads!" said Mark.

"Exactly," said *Margarita*, "and for me to come to this understanding was when ... when I finally had the courage to not be afraid or ashamed of these feelings I've had inside of me for all these years for this wonderful gorgeous man!"

"Me, gorgeous?" said Joe. "Well, yes, I guess in a way you're right. Because being with you, I see that the whole world is gorgeous! For over 20 years I was attached to our Marines and I saw action. I was there beside our boys as they were dying. And yet I can tell you it takes more courage to admit and accept these feelings that we carry within us than to go to war.

"WAR IS EASY COMPARED TO THESE TENDER FEELINGS WE CARRY INSIDE OF US! Since kids we play war games! We see war movies! Football included! Which leads us to be more and more frightened to open our hearts, until there with our last dying breath, we can't run away from our true feelings anymore. So yes, I entirely agree with Vic, that the only reason we're here on earth is to give Birth to God. Can't you feel it? Muslim, Jew, Hindu, Christian, Atheist, it doesn't matter. We all have this little feeling within us that we have something inside of us that we need to share with the world!"

"Do you think that this is why our major religions were all started by men?" asked Matt.

"Yes, I'm beginning to see that," said Joe.

"Then this makes sense why men are so willing to die or kill for their religions, because it's their child."

"YES, YOU GOT IT!" shouted Joe. "And this is why I've been feeling so stupid and ridiculous all these years until Vic told us that Giving Birth To God is why we come to earth!

"Suddenly I knew why his book *Rain of Gold* had moved me as no other book has ever done! *Rain* isn't a history book about just family and war and coming from Mexico to the United States. No, it's about people Giving Birth To God with all their Hearts and Souls, through hard times, through good times, every day by greeting the sunrise as the Right Eye of God and every flower and bird as a Miracle of Beauty given to us by the Almighty."

"And clouds of butterflies!" added a nun.

"Yes, and clouds of butterflies and happy children laughing and playing and their BEAUTIFUL VOICES ECHOING THROUGHOUT THE CANYON!"

I took in a deep breath, and I now suddenly knew why Joe was a cross-dresser and why he'd only been able to beat men who were abusive to their wives and kids when he was dressed as a woman. Simply, in wanting to be heroes, in wanting to give Birth to God, men had to actually first give life to these women-like-feelings they'd been carrying within themselves since ever!

"My God," Joe was now saying, "look at me. I'm the one who never ever speaks," he said, with tears coming to his eyes. "Move boulders, yes! Get right into the front lines of combat, yes! But talk, no, no, never, until now that I have this beautiful lady's hand in my hand, a hand that I've only dreamed of holding one day," he said, bringing *Margarita's* hand to his lips and kissing it. "I love you, my dear," he added.

"And I love you," she said, taking his huge thick hand to her own lips and kissing it.

"Okay," I now said, "let's now take each other's hands. Right hand, our heart hand, facing up for receiving, and our left hand, facing down, for flooding our whole Mother Earth with Love*Amor*, who's no larger than a grain of sand on the Seashore of Creation! This is what *mi Mama* would do with her little mango tree at 3 every afternoon, and we, too, can do this globally every afternoon, helping give Birth to God that's the best within each of us. Breathe. Breathe. And now kiss each other's hand as we saw Joe and *Margarita* do, and then place both of your hands over your heart and close your eyes, giving a chance for your Heart*Corazon* to Gift Life to Your Soul!"

Everyone was cooperating. We'd come a long ways.

"Good, good," I said, "and now let's each of us ask God, with our own Heartfelt words, for guidance as . . . as we COLLECTIVELY LEAP into the Unknown of moving Our Sacred Mother Church from Rome to Ireland, where we will have OUR FIRST LADY POPE!"

And there was silence.

Respectful, Relaxed, Joyful Silence as we each asked for guidance with our own words. Then here came Jesus once again smelling of Wild Flowers, spinning through us with *gusto*, assisting us in Giving Birth To Our Collective Spirit Of God-Goding after so many 10s of 1000s of years of ALL, ALL, ALL OF US BEING PREGNANT WITH HOLY SPIRIT!

AWOMAN!

ACHILDREN!

AMEN!

BOOK FOUR

THIRTEEN

The next day I was taken back to the airport by the same driver who had picked me up. He asked me how it had gone and I didn't know how to even begin. Finally, I just said, "It went very well, especially this morning. You see, they'd had a chance to sleep on what we'd covered, and oh, my God, had they transformed!" I laughed. "If we'd been able to keep going for a week, I'm sure we would've reached the level of being able to create rain like my grandmothers were able to do when they were dying of thirst as they came north through the Mexico Revolution."

"Your grandmothers were able to create rain?"

"Well, not really create," I said, "but summon rain. You see, all people all over the world used to know how to do this or else we could never have survived as a species for all these 100s of 1000s of years. We don't have fur like a bear. We don't have claws like a lion. So we were given the ability to be Miracle Makers. This is all well documented in my trilogy *Rain of Gold*, and especially in *Wild Steps of Heaven* which I strongly recommend that people read last."

"I'll be, very interesting. Sounds like something I'd like to read."

And he asked no more questions and I was glad, because what more could I have said to him, told him that Collectively we'd moved into Our Guardian Angel Psychic Powers and we hadn't just "seen" our Future. No, we'd actually manifested Our Global Future, and so yes, it was already written in the Stars that the Vatican had, indeed, relocated to Ireland where we'd had Our First Lady Pope.

Also, I guess, I could've told him that by April 14, 2052 there will be no more wars in the world. By then, conflicts will

be—not fought or negotiated—but dissolved before they can solid-
ify into emotional-manifestation and this will be primarily done by
Grandmothers and Great Grandmothers.

I was quiet the rest of our drive to the airport and then in
Chicago, where I was changing planes, a storm came in and we were
told we'd have about a five to six-hour layover. I decided to just relax,
find a quiet corner, stretch out on the floor, and take a nap. Up ahead
two little girls were running in the aisle and laughing and playing.

"Hi, girls!" I said. They stopped playing. They were about four
and five. "I want you young women to Know you are Angels. You
really are, and you're wonderful, and you came into this world with
Total Recall, and so you're in charge. Because, you see, your parents
also came in as Angels, but then they got stressed out and all confused, so they quickly forgot they are Angels, too, and so you need
to re-teach them. Have a good life," I added, tipping my Stetson to
them and I kept going.

Up ahead, I found a quiet corner by the huge windows facing
the runway of incoming and outgoing planes. I put my backpack
down, slipped off my western boots, and put my Stetson on top of
them so the colorful boots now looked like a very short cowboy.
Then I lay down on the floor, stretched out my arms and legs,
closed my eyes, and was just relaxing and going to sleep when I felt
a presence to the right of me.

I opened my eyes and turned to look and saw that here stood
those two little girls with two more little girls and an older boy who
was probably about eight years old, and they were just staring at
me, and not moving and/or saying anything. Then it came to me.

"Oh, yeah," I said, "I'd like all of you to Know you are Angels.
You really are, and so you came into this world Knowing everything there is to Know. And so you are wonderful and fantastic, and
your Angel Voice comes to your head from here in your heart," I
said, patting my heart area, "And this is your genius, your Voice of
Genius, and so you young people are in charge, because your parents
have forgotten they are Angels, too, and so you need to re-educate
them and let them Know they are also Angels and wonderful. In

fact," I added, "you guys still have cellular memory that your arms are really wings. So go ahead, spread out your Angel-Arm-Wings, and KNOW THAT YOU ARE WONDERFUL AND FULL OF MAGIC!"

And so they did, they spread out their Angel-Arms and began flying around me screeching with joy and *gusto*!

"WONDERFUL! Great! And now I need to get some sleep, so please just go back to your parents, but don't forget, you're in charge and you are really, really ANGELS AND FULL OF WONDER!"

They flew around me a couple of more times, and then they flew off and I took in a few deep breaths, put my Stetson over my eyes, and went right to sleep. And I was dreaming of my horse Casanova and Buccaneer Beach and smelling Wild Flowers when someone kicked the bottom of my left foot.

But I just ignored it and kept sleeping until they kicked me again and this kick was much harder. I opened my eyes, took the Stetson off my face, and I saw there was a tall girl just beyond my feet. She was maybe 10 or 11 years old and she was staring at me and all about her were these smaller, shorter kids. About 10 of them. And they, too, were just staring at me.

Well, I sat up, brought my water bottle out of my backpack, drank, then told them the same thing that I'd already said two times before, and when I finished they didn't go away. No, they stayed all around me flapping their arms like wings, and then here came some more kids, and some more, and then I noticed that their parents were coming, too, and when one father grabbed his little four year old girl to take her away, she jerked loose from him with power and yelled, "NO! I'M AN ANGEL!" And she came back to be with the other children with her arms out like wings and her whole face was full of joy!

The father rushed in at me. His whole face was red with rage.

"WHO ARE YOU? What have you done to our children!" he shouted.

And I could now see that he wasn't alone. There were about a dozen other parents all staring at me, too. I got up off the floor. I had no idea what to say and/or do. I closed my eyes, rubbed my face, took in several deep breaths, and once more I caught the scent of Wild Flowers, and when I opened my eyes here was Jesus with his Sacred Holy Arms outstretched, too, and He was laughing and spinning around and around with also the JOY OF A CHILD!

I laughed. His laughter was contagious, but I could also see that this angry father in front of me didn't think that this was a laughing situation.

"Look," I said, still smiling with *gusto*, "I'm a writer and … and, well, we're doing research at the University of Houston in conjunction with Yale on children having Total Recall Of Being Angels. You see, children are nowadays coming into the world with a way more advanced understanding of how the Universe really works than us older people. We adults basically still live in the dark ages of the illusion that the world is flat, time is linear, and that there is separation. But these kids, who are now coming into manifestation, Cellularly Know that all of Creation is Interconnected, and so they're not fear-based, and instead are FREE TO BE GENIUSING ANGELS! Just look at them, they're so happy, because they Know, just like a rose Knows how to Be a rose, that they are actually OPEN, LOVING, HAPPY HUMAN BEINGS OF LIGHT, JUST LIKE EINSTEIN," I said, thinking this explanation would calm him down. But it didn't.

"Do you have proof?" he barked angrily.

"Proof of what?" I asked.

"Proof that you're not a crackpot!"

"Oh, yeah, sure," I said, "in my backpack I have a copy of my National Best Seller *Rain of Gold,* and some great articles written about me in the *New York Times*, the *L.A. Times, Chicago Tribune, People Magazine* and a bunch of others. Here, let me get them out and show them to you."

"No! You don't have to do that! I just want my child to come back with me. You had no right!"

"You mean you're upset because I told your child that she's an Angel and a Genius and Wonderful?"

"Well, no, I'm not offended by that," he said. "I'm offended by her not obeying me and … and … I don't need to be explaining myself to you! She's my child!"

And I almost said, "Not really. She's God-Goding's child and she's her own Human Angel Person," but I decided this wouldn't be the best thing to say, especially since all the other parents were looking at me with concern, too. So I turned to the kids.

"All right, you Geniusing Angels," I said. "Please, all of you go back to your parents, but remember you're in charge, because you're—"

"My little girl IS NOT IN CHARGE!" yelled the angry father.

But the mother only laughed. "Oh, come on, honey, you know she is," she said. "Thank you very much," she said, turning to me.

A couple of the kids came up and hugged me, and one little boy put his shoes into my boots, fell over, but then got up and his whole face was in ecstasy as he tried walking off wearing my boots that came up past his knees.

People started laughing.

"Can we get your books at any bookstore?" someone asked.

"Yeah, sure, of course, *Rain of Gold* is a trilogy, but my young adult book is *Walking Stars*, a bunch of short stories, and the first one is titled *The Smartest Human I Ever Met, My Brother's Dog Shep.* Pets are so important for kids. They teach love and caretaking and responsibility. Check out my children's books. That's where education really begins. Thank you. Thank you very much, and I'm really sorry if I upset you."

The tall girl stayed behind.

"Yes?" I said.

"Thank you," she said. "I just knew that there was more to life."

And saying this she began to Glow with Golden Light, then she turned and took off running, and I heard Jesus say within me, "She's Our Third Lady Pope!"

"Really?"

"Yes, really."

"Oh, my God! Thank You, Jesus."

"Thank you, Victor."

And hearing this, I began to laugh and the whole entire place filled with the beautiful fragrance of Wild Flowers! I lay back down, closed my eyes, put my Stetson over my face and went back to sleep. Oh, some of those parents had truly looked all bent out of shape, and who could blame them. Their kids had been Aglow with Golden Light just like that tall girl and they hadn't been able to see it. Only the kids could see and feel each other's Glowing Holy Light of Love*Amor.*

Oh, I could hardly wait to get home so I could go across the grass and past the chicken coops to tell my mother what had happened. She'd been absolutely right. Coming to see these retired—I mean Inspired—nuns and priests had been the most important talk I'd ever given in my life, especially when I'd shared with them the story of my mother's mango tree after dinner.

My God, they'd immediately all gotten it.

Yes, with Our First Lady Pope, women were going to start remembering how for 100s of 1000s of years they'd been the caretakers of the Sacred Seeds of Our Holy Garden as we'd migrated around Our Beloved Mother Earth, and so it hadn't taken 1000s of years for our gardens to acclimate to new weather zones as science liked to say. No, it had only taken one generation of a woman singing and giving Love*Amor* to Our Sacred Holy Garden just as my mother had done with our beloved mango tree.

And the nuns had instantly understood this.

Yes, in One Great Mighty Stroke, Women—Women of Substance from all over Our Beloved Mother Earth—were going to come forward and activate the Sacred Holy Dormant Stardust Seeds that we Human People have been carrying within us for 100s of 1,000s of years, if not millions!

This is what happened on Our Six Sister Planets!

This was how they, who were even more lost and violent than us, were finally able to come into Harmony with the Symphony of Creation Creating, then establish Peace and Abundance for All on each of their planets and … and also this is why Our Star Cousins were now all rooting for us!

YES! YES! YES!

For in the first 100 years of this Global Transformation of Our Collective Consciousness, the Music of Enya, who carries the Soul of Ireland within her, is going to echo around the world off mountaintops and across valleys AND TO THE STARS, OUR TRUE HOME! And hence germinate within ALL, ALL, ALL WOMEN, the Sacred Knowledge that gave my mother the Wisdom how to Love and Sing to her mango seed that was so far from home.

And by November 10, 2026 at 3 pm California Time all the Sacred Seeds for World Harmony and Peace and Abundance for All will be planted for the next 26,000 years of Balanced Feminine Compassionate Energy, meaning balanced passion in common between men and women.

Oh, I could hardly wait to have another *quesadilla* just off the hot *comal* with *mi Mama*, so I could then give her the little antique French crystal glass that I'd brought home for her.

OH, MIRACLE MAKERS are we!

DREAMCATCHERS are we!

SONGSHIFTERS are we!

And never in a billion years had I ever thought I could go on such a FANTASTIC VOYAGEDREAM OF TOTAL TRANSFORMATION!

It was DONE!

It was COMPLETED!

In one great mighty leap, OUR FIRST LADY POPE HAS ALREADY UNITED ALL THE WOMEN OF THE WORLD, and so we are right on schedule, and by 2052 April 14th there will be no more wars, and armies will instead be used as "wings'; as Angel Arms, for helping Human People Globally to clean up our disaster areas and—OH, HEAVEN ON EARTH WILL NOW BE OUR NORM! Just as it happened on Our Six Sister Planets eons and eons of Timeless Time ago!

YES! YES! YES!
IT HAS ALL, ALL, ALL FINALLY FINISHED IN BEAUTY,
AS HARRY WALTERS EXPLAINED TO ME!
ACHILDREN!
AWOMEN!
AMEN!

COOKIES

AND WARM MILK

And so after my talk in Wisconsin in the late 1990s, I was invited to speak at many world peace organizations, convents, churches, libraries, grammar schools, high schools, universities, and convention centers all across the country. Then in Kentucky at Our Mother of God Church, after I gave my talk and I was having a *tequila* with a group of nuns at an ultra-modern bar and restaurant, I met this feisty happy little nun who radiated such power and confidence that I bluntly asked her right out if she'd like to be Our First Lady Pope. And without hesitation, she said:

"SURE! WHY NOT?"

WE ALL BURST OUT LAUGHING, and another nun said:

"And she'll make a great Lady Pope! She's brilliant, and she bakes the best chocolate chip cookies in all the world, and, I tell you, it's going to take a lot of cookies to put a smile on people's faces and make this a kinder, sweeter world!"

I couldn't stop laughing. "Then this will be our first business at hand after moving our Church from Rome to Ireland?" I asked.

"Certainly!" said another nun. "What else can help move people's hearts more quickly than the best-tasting chocolate chip cookies in all the world?"

"And warm milk," added another nun.

"You're right," I said. "You're absolutely right, and only women could've come up with this! OH, WOW! So then it's in the bag! Our First Lady Pope and then World Harmony and Peace and—not

just Abundance—BUT CHOCOLATE CHIP COOKIES AND
WARM MILK FOR ALL!"
And so there you have it.
Not complicated.
Not pushy.
Not revolutionary in the typical sense of the word, but oh, so
downright tasty!

Thank you, *gracias,*
Victor E. Villaseñor

OUR
INTERPLANETARY
MUSICAL

I AWOKE LAUGHING!
I AWOKE HOWLING WITH *CARCJADAS,* meaning big belly-shaking laughter! Oh, it was WONDERFUL! I was down at the Oceanside pier wearing bright red baggy pants like a clown and banging a rock and a trash can lid together and looking a lot like Johnny Depp, singing so far off key that the Cats ran away with their tails straight up in the air and the Dogs lay down and covered their ears with their paws, then they, too, all began singing, HOWLING AND MEOWING TO THE HIGH HEAVENS!

Kids loved it, and began to sing along with me and the Cats and Dogs. And other Kids began going through the trash cans as they'd seen me do earlier and now they, too, with a couple of Homeless People, began making homemade musical instruments from the sticks and cans and boards and trash.

And sure enough without anyone telling them, the Kids and Homeless People took the lead and I followed infront as we danced our way out to the end of the long, beautiful Oceanside pier. We were having a grand time, and seeing us coming people grinned and stepped aside, but then some other people began to join us.

Oh, we'd started out with only about a dozen Kids and two Homeless People and me, and now as we came around the end of the pier, we had well over 200 People plus a dozen Dogs who were howling and jumping about and another dozen Cats who were prancing with their tails straight up in the air in perfect harmony with our music!

And this was when the Dolphins began leaping out of the sea, making birdlike chirping high-pitched sounds, and the Surfers, who were catching waves, began singing and dancing, too. By the time we approached the shoreline there was well over 1,000 People ready to receive Our Happy Wild Music and a couple of 100 Cats and Dogs cheering us on!

OH, IT WAS BEAUTIFUL! BEAUTIFUL! BEAUTIFUL!

Then we were singing and dancing across a luscious green meadow, oh, so different than the dry semi-desert of Southern California; and...and then all these Little Green People began sprouting out of the wildflowers. Dancing and laughing, these Little Green People joined right in with the Kids leading, and then we stopped. Just like that, we stopped. Out in the middle of the luscious green meadow, we stopped.

No more Singing.

No more Laughter.

All was Silent.

And then...and then here came one single note.

One clear single note. And then one more clear single note, and then the Holy Voice of a Woman came softly, softly across the meadow as if...this Holy Sacred Feminine Voice was coming from the very depths of Our Holy Mother Earth.

And at first, I didn't recognize her.

No, I'd never heard a voice of such clarity and Heart and Soul. And then it hit me like a Lightning Bolt! IT WAS ENYA!

ENYA! ENYA! THE MUSICAL SOUL OF IRELAND!

And we, in the luscious green meadow, stood TRANSFIXED!

Not moving!

Not breathing!

And her Heartfelt Music engulfed us like a sea of Feelings, Gifting Living Life to Our Collective Soul, and then...and then right there before us, we witnessed THE GREAT ILLUMINATING

GATES OF HEAVEN OPEN WIDE AND WE ALL BEGAN SINGING IN HARMONY!

We, who'd sang so horribly, now sang as ONE UNITED WONDEROUS VOICE, as we danced, danced, DANCED TOWARDS THE HOLY GATES!

And so from ALL FOUR CORNERS OF THE WORLD WE CAME!

1,000s OF US!

10s of 1,000s OF US!

100s of 1,000s OF US!

1,000,000s OF US!

10s OF MILLIONS OF US!

100s OF MILLIONS OF US!

And the Children and Women and Homeless were leading and we Knew no fear. For we were all OPEN, OPEN, OPEN OF HEART AND ALIVE OF SOUL!

YOU, ME, WE, ALL OF US WERE OPEN OF HEART AND ALIVE OF SOUL AND BIG BIG HAPPY as we joyfully passed through the Holy Gates, becoming Snow Geese Human Angels of Ourselves, and this was when we all began smelling cookies.

CHOCOLATE CHIP COOKIES!

THE BEST CHOCOLATE CHIP COOKIES IN ALL THE WORLD!

And our eyes got HUGE! Our mouths began to water, and then—OH, WOW! — magically we each had a chocolate chip cookie and a large glass of warm milk in hand.

I AWOKE LAUGHING!

HOWLING WITH *CARCAJADAS* and still tasting the best chocolate chip cookie in all the world! Then I kind of remembered that we'd all been speaking in the sing-song feminine language of Gaelic, and we'd realized that we'd all finally ... come home.

Yes, oh, yes, Ireland had once more saved Western Civilization from extinction!

I smiled!

I laughed!

It was DONE!

It was FINISHED IN BEAUTY!

It had really, really already happened and so we are now on our way, having left behind 26,000 years of Out-Of-Balance Aggressive Masculine Energy and moving into 26,000 years of Balanced Compassionate Feminine Energy!

We are not alone.

And we have never been alone.

We belong to 6 Sister Planets and we used to have a Twin Sister Mother Earth planet that was all but destroyed by Human People eons of Timeless Time ago. She, along with our own Beloved Mother Earth, had been the 'Hawaii' of our 6 Sister Planets where our Star Cousins used to love to come vacationing, and so now our Cousins are, indeed, very anxious for us to AWAKEN once again. So we can help heal our Beloved Mother Earth, get ourselves off the Most Endangered List, and then they'll be able to continue vacationing on our Hawaii-like planet for millions of years!

Yes, we are not alone, and we have never been alone.

How do you think that we ever managed to come up with all these fantastic great breakthroughs in travel and communications in the last 100 years?

From horse to automobile, to airplane and jets, then to the moon!

From smoke signals and telegraphs to landlines to cell phones and computers!

From stage productions to silent movies to talking films to T.V. to Facebook, Instagram, Twitter, etc.!

From school and church musicals to gigantic global musical events!

All these are gifts given to us by Our Star Cousins, and now, now that they have helped us to realize world-wide communications, Our Star Cousins are ready to assist us in an Interplanetary Musical just as they'd been prepared to do 78,000 years ago, but we hadn't been Spiritually ready to 'receive' back then.

NO JOKE!

Back then we hadn't been ready to 'receive', but now we are.

Now we are Godelutionary right on schedule to 'receive' and Transform from Masculine Energy back to Feminine Energy, and then 26,000 years in the Future to Transform from Feminine Energy back to Masculine Energy, and so forth for the next 10 million years!

Pretty good, eh?

And now I'd like all of you, who've DreamVoyaged with us so far, to face the person to the right or left of you, place your hands behind your back, bend forward and gently touch your foreheads together. Then look into each other's eyes. Really look deeply into each other's eyes, and most of you will see that your eyes are ... are Golden.

And if all your life you've thought your eyes are blue, just go outside and face the early morning sunlight and have someone look into your eyes and tell you what color they are. You'll be surprised, because they will tell you your eyes have little specks of reddish-gold around your pupils. And as you get older and older, your eyes will become more and more golden, just as it happened to Blue-Eyed Shirley MacLaine, who, of course, became more and more Spiritually Conscious the older she became.

And if you've always assumed your eyes are dark brown or solid black, have a person look deeper into your eyes, past the first layer, and they will see that the second layer is golden. In fact, SOLID GOLD! And if you think your eyes are hazel or brown, ask the person to blink their own eyes and look again, and they will tell you that your eyes are SOLID GOLD, TOO!

Why?

Because Golden-Eyed People are part of our Larger Indigenous Grand Plan, when every 26,000 years Our Collective Consciousness Shapeshifts, Songshifts, and Globally Human People ReAwaken to their Original Instructions, and Regain Total Recall of 100s of 1,000s of years, if not millions, and Life becomes a Rain of Gold!

And, also, look at magazines and you'll see that most models are no longer blue-eyed like way back in Frank Sinatra and Paul Newman and Doris Day and Shirley MacLaine's day. No, now most male and female models and celebrities have Golden Eyes, and … and no one seems to have noticed.

Also, I'd like you to know that that tall little girl at the airport in Chicago, who told me she'd thought there was more to life, had Golden Eyes, and remember, Jesus told me that she will be Our Third Lady Pope.

AND SO I AWOKE LAUGHING!

LAUGHING WITH *CARCAJADAS!* And in my DreamVoyage I'd been wearing bright baggy red pants, a bright yellow-golden shirt, a big Stetson hat, tall turquoise cowboy boots, and I'd been following infront with all the Children and Homeless People leading out to the end of the Oceanside pier. Then magically—OH, WOW! We'd Transformed to Ireland where we passed through the ILLUMINATING GATES OF HEAVEN, BECOMING SNOW GEESE ANGELS OF OURSELVES!

Enya calling! Calling! CALLING! WELCOMING US!

Carole King singing "A Natural Woman".

Joan Baez singing "We Shall Overcome".

Then Louie Armstrong, with that great big smile of his, singing "Hello, Dolly" for the inauguration of Our First Lady Pope.

And here she comes, Our First Lady Pope, looking a lot like that feisty little old nun from Our Mother of God Church and Convent in Kentucky, and she's moving in the Style and Grace of THE GIRL FROM IPANEMA!

OH, WOW!

And she's surrounded by Angels and Children with Jesus grinning and spinning all through them with HIS WONDEROUS SCENT OF WILDFLOWERS!

And Mary, the Mother of God, takes Our First Lady Pope's hand and leads her through the Holy Gates and into the Other Side of Living Life which is, of course, the exact same Green Luscious Meadow where Little Green People are sprouting out of tall grass and flowers, and wild songbirds are flying about in all directions, and bees are kissing the wildflowers, and butterflies are floating all about in abundance, and Snow Geese, Canadian Honkers, African Geese are all flying in V-Formations, cackling and honking their heads off!

THEN WE SEE IT!

We see the gorgeous cute little old Church at the far end of the meadow, and our feisty little old First Lady Pope keeps smiling, keeps dancing that world-famous Brazilian dance of Bosa Nova Music of the last mid-century and ... and the Songbirds and Bees and Butterflies surround her as she comes up the Luscious Green Meadow towards the little Church, passing fields of sheep and cattle and Shetland ponies, who are ALL, ALL, ALL watching her with GREAT INTENT!

Then when she reaches the steps of Our Little Church, a tiny cute baby lamb comes rushing up to Our First Lady Pope, BLEATING HER HEAD OFF. Our Feisty Little Lady Pope bends down and picks up the lost little lamb, soothing her head and kissing her; then with baby lamb in hand, she turns to take her First Official Step into Our Church for THE NEXT 100 YEARS!

Can you see it?

Can you feel it?

Can you SEE-FEEL IT deep within your own WOMB OF CREATION—for now you Know, without a shadow of a doubt, that You, Me, We, All of Us, along with Our First Lady Pope, are GIVING BIRTH TO GOD-GODING!

OH, YES! YES! YES!

JUST LOOK UP! LOOK UP! HERE THEY COME!

INDIGO CHILDREN!

GOLDEN-EYED CHILDREN!

HARRY POTTER CHILDREN! FROM EVERY TRIBE AND EVERY CORNER OF OUR WHOLE MOTHER EARTH!

And they're aboard Harry Potter's magic rainbow-colored CHOO-CHOO train, blaring its horn as it STREAMS ACROSS THE HEAVENS AND THROUGH THE CLOUDS!

J.K. Rowling is the conductor and she's wearing a great big rainbow-colored hat and pulling the cord for the train's BLARING HORN at every stop, where EVEN MORE CHILDREN QUICKLY RUSH ABOARD!

And at each stop Oprah and a group of Happy, Smiling Nuns are holding platters of the biggest best-tasting CHOCOLATE CHIP COOKIES IN ALL THE WORLD, and the Queen of Spain and the Queen of England are handing out large mugs of warm milk.

Then once more J.K. Rowling pulls the cord of the big shiny brass horn and the rainbow-colored CHOO-CHOO train GOES SHOOTING THROUGH THE CLOUDS AND ACROSS THE HEAVENS, and the Kids are grinning, laughing, waving flags, and munching on THE BEST CHOCOLATE CHIP COOKIES IN ALL THE WORLD!

Also, aboard are our 13 Indigenous Grandmothers from around the world and they are telling age-old stories of Real Magic and the Power of Women. And Felicitas D. Goodman, Clarissa Pinkola Estes, Louise Hay, and Anita Diamant, who have penned some of the most influential books of all time, are aboard, too!

OH, OUR COLORFUL CHOO-CHOO TRAIN IS PACKED FULL OF CHILDREN AND WOMEN WHO HAVE AWAKENED!

100s of them!

1,000s of them!

100s of 1,000s of them!

Millions of them from all over OUR BELOVED MOTHER EARTH!

Then here comes Pope Francis himself, accompanied by Madonna and Lady Gaga—two very good Italian women—and they are DANCING AND SINGING as they come across THE HEAVENS TO ENYA'S WELCOMING HEARTSOUL MUSIC OF IRELAND!

And ... and now Our First Lady Pope walks up the Three Holy Steps of Our New Vatican of the Catholic Church, leading the whole Christian World back to the Basics of Faith and Love and

Hope, Reverence and Respect and Compassion, with the Total Understanding that we're ALL, ALL, ALL EQUALLY CHILDREN OF GOD-GODING.

Our First Lady Pope passes through the entrance of our little old Church with the baby lamb in her arms and the place is packed full of People. Some dressed in work clothes and others all dressed up. Everyone gets to their feet and many have tears of joy streaming down their faces. Some hold infants in their arms. Others hold large bundles of flowers. And still others have baskets of vegetables and fruit that they'd brought from their own gardens. And one little old couple hold their beautiful red hen and a basket full of eggs.

And the Scent of WILDFLOWERS permeates the whole place!

Suddenly, the little lamb lets out an ear-piercing BLEATING CALL, and leaps out of Our First Lady Pope's arms, rushing to her mother, who's at someone's side inside of the Church and our little lamb instantly begins to nurse.

People laugh and applaud and Our First Lady Pope now comes down the center aisle blessing all the Offerings that People have brought to their New Vatican.

And as the People part, we are now able to see the Holy Altar and … and Jesus isn't hanging on a cross. OH, NO! He and His Blessed Mother are sitting down and smiling and They are surrounded by Angels and Happy Adoring Children from every Tribe from all around the whole world. And these Kids have dolls and baby ducks and rabbits and goats and sheep in their arms, and one Child has a little kangaroo. They, too, have brought their own offerings.

And outside of Our Holy Little Church, millions upon millions of People are still coming up the long luscious green valley, and now we see SPACESHIPS. And they are SHOOTING! SWOOPING! SOMERSAULTING ALL THROUGH THE HEAVENS!

WE HAVE ARRIVED!

WE HAVE ALL! ALL! ALL FINALLY REALLY ARRIVED!

WE HAVE ALL! ALL! ALL FINALLY REACHED THE HIGHEST VIBRATIONAL FREQUENCIES OF

UNCONDITIONAL LOVE*AMOR,* and so we can now See-Feel the Eternal Presence of Our Star Cousins as we, Collectively, take our First Official Global Step Towards HARMONY AND PEACE AND ABUNDANCE FOR ALL!

Then, out of the blue, here comes Whoopi Goldberg!

OH, YES! YES! YES, WHOOPI! And she's driving a Winged White Horse-drawn GLOWING GOLDEN CHARIOT, flying among the Spaceships, and at her side is Pope Francis himself, and they're LAUGHING THEIR HEADS OFF WITH *CARCAJADAS*—WHOOPING IT ALL UP!

ACHILDREN!

AWOMEN!

AMEN!

And now Our First Lady Pope goes up to the altar, genuflects, and makes the sign of the cross over herself as she faces Jesus, our Children, and Our Most Holy Blessed Mother Mary. Then she turns and goes up to the podium, signals everyone to please be seated, and she starts to speak. Calmly. Gently. Slowly.

"Welcome," she says. "Welcome to Our Beloved Mother Church of Jesus Christ that is now going to be at last led by women from all different cultures from all around the globe for the next 50,000 years. Yes, 50,000 years! And we thank Enya, for keeping the fires of Ireland's Heart and Soul alive all these years, and we give thanks to Lady Gaga and Madonna for escorting Pope Francis, Our Beloved Last Pope in Rome, through the Heavens and guided by God's Symphony Full of Hope and Love and Healing for all of us and our most precious Mother Earth. Thank you, Ladies—Enya, Lady Gaga, and Madonna, and, of course, we thank you, Pope Francis!"

With his typical grand smile, Pope Francis waves to everyone and . . . and Our First Lady Pope takes in several deep breaths before continuing.

"Also, I'd like to give thanks to all my fellow Nuns and Priests and Brothers and Bishops and Cardinals who have joined us. For Ours isn't a movement of destruction; rather, it is, in fact, a Movement of Fulfillment!"

She stops once again and takes a few more deep breaths.

"Also, my warmest thanks to J.K. Rowling for all her years of uncompromising development of a whole global generation of children who are open to embrace magic," she now says. "For without these children, who many are adults now, we would not be here today...at this great monumental event of the changing of the guard for ALL OF HUMANITY!"

Once more she stops and breathes, then glances around before continuing.

"Also, especially I'd like to thank Oprah and Queen Elizabeth of England and Queen Letizia of Spain, who have become close friends of mine over the last year just like J.K. Rowling, who, by the way, they now all know my recipe for chocolate chip cookies to the letter, realizing that our most important ingredient is...is Love. LOTS AND LOTS OF LOVE, which, as you can guess, is also going to be the most important ingredient of Our Church in Ireland for the next 100 years.

"And I'd like to also thank Carole King and Joan Baez, who've also become close friends of mine, and then the great indestructible Louie Armstrong, who spontaneously came to us from the Other Side of Living, for the sole purpose of INSPIRING US WITH HIS GREAT ENERGIZING 'HELLO, DOLLY!' Oh, I once more felt like a young school girl dancing up the valley with the grace and movement of the GIRL FROM IPANEMA! OH, MY!"

Saying this, she now bursts with laughter, doing a little quick-stepping movement with her arms up in the air, then she says, "Okay, now, moving onto Our First Official Business, I'd like all of you to turn on your cell phones, if you haven't already done so, and record what I am about to share with you, and...and then please send it out to the WHOLE WORLD! TO ALL YOUR FRIENDS AND FAMILY! And not just to Catholics and ex-Catholics! For this message is for all of HUMANITY! And Our Official First Statement is that I, your First Lady Pope, and all other Popes, both male and female, from this day on for the next 50,000 years, are not—do you hear me—ARE NOT INFALLIBLE!"

People are shocked.

They don't know what to think, or feel, or say, or do. The infallibility of the Pope of Rome had always been the foundation of the whole Catholic indoctrination, so that then no one could question anything that the Pope proclaimed had come to him, and only to him, straight from God.

People glanced around, looking at each other, and then slowly it begins to register what this means that Our First Lady Pope has said, and now THE PEOPLE EXPLODE WITH APPLAUSE!

Our First Lady Pope sees the Blessed Holy Light of God-Goding come into the People with the SPINNING, SPINNING WILDFLOWER SCENT OF JESUS-GENIUSING DIRECTLY INTO THEIR HEARTS AND SOULS, and hence, Activating their HOLY VOICE WITHIN!

Tears of joy stream down Our First Lady Pope's face as she reaches into the left sleeve of her loose-fitting white robe, bringing out the little white handkerchief that her Irish grandmother had given her 70-some years ago, when she'd decided to take her vows to become the bride of Our Lord Jesus Christ.

Her grandmother Sarah had been blind but still...she'd managed to hand embroider tiny red and yellow flowers and even more tiny green leaves into the white Irish linen handkerchief that...that Our First Lady Pope had not used until this day. This day that she'd only dreamed of. This day that she'd kept in secret ever since Jesus had come and asked her for her hand in marriage on her 16th birthday.

She can't stop crying.

Tears of joy just keep streaming down her face and she can feel the presence of Jesus and her grandmother at her side along with her mother, and, of course, Mary, the Mother of God.

She giggles.

Oh, she can still remember how the bishops and cardinals had been against her fellow nuns when they'd wished to name their Church and Convent in Kentucky the Mother of God. Oh, if only those bishops and cardinals were alive today and could...could witness what was now happening!

Oh, she can't stop laughing and giggling—she's so happy! BIG BIG HAPPY! She and her fellow nuns had certainly come a long ways in the last couple of 100 years, and … and …

"And so I'd like all of you to know," she now says, "why my fellow Lady Bishops and Cardinals have unanimously decided, through the Spirit and Holy Guidance of Jesus and Mary, that … that all Popes from this day forth will no longer be considered infallible. Because, it is you … you, me, we, all of us, the People—of the People, by the People, for the People, who are INFALLIBLE!"

The place EXPLODES!

This, the People can HEAR!

This, the People can UNDERSTAND!

This, they instantly Know is Uniting them Directly to God! In every form! In every name! In every faith! In every way throughout the WHOLE WORLD for they are, indeed, ALL! ALL! ALL PEOPLE—of the People, by the People, for the People since ever, and now, at long last, they are Being Acknowledged for who THEY REALLY ARE!

THE PLACE CONTINUES EXPLODING!

EXPLODING with applause and cheers and ear-piercing whistles!

And this message of Our First Lady goes viral around the whole world, rocking the very foundation of the cute little Church, and sending a 300 FEET TIDAL WAVE OF GIVING BIRTH TO GOD-GODING THOUGHOUT … THROUGHOUT ALL! ALL! ALL OF HUMANITY!

And outside of our cute little Church and further down the Luscious Green Meadow, Spaceships are now landing and our Star Cousins are coming off their Spacecrafts as Light Beings, then quickly ShapeShifting, SongShifting into Human People Form as they come among their Mother Earth Cousins, also celebrating this long awaited Shift of Human Being Consciousness that … almost occurred 78,000 years ago, but didn't.

And with cell phones turned up, everyone across the entire valley and around the Whole World can hear Our First Lady Pope's

Words and see that the Spaceships have, indeed, landed and that their inhabitants have joined in with Humanity.

"And proceeding in this same vein," Our First Lady Pope continues, "I'd like to announce that secondly, without fear or judgment, and instead Total Faith and Trust in God, and that also from this day forward, we are Activating the full and real definition of what the word catholic really means in … in accordance to the Webster New World Dictionary of the American Language, which states—"

She pauses.

She pauses and glances around and all is silent. In fact, it seems like even the sheep and cows and Shetland ponies are attentive.

"Which states: universal; all-inclusive, of general interest or value; hence having broad sympathies and understanding; liberal."

Her whole face begins GLOWING!

People see this and make the sign of the cross over themselves. Others glance downward—her Glowing Holy Light is so Bright!

"Did you hear me? LIBERAL!" she repeats. "A word that has taken on negative meaning in the last few years. And yet, I ask you, where would we be today if we hadn't liberated slavery? Where would my family of true hillbilly Kentuckians be if the People, by the People, of the People, for the People hadn't liberated ourselves from the British Empire? And where would women be today, if they hadn't gotten the right to vote!

"LIBERTY! LIBERTY! LIBERY! Is the very foundation of progress and … and our guarantee that good things will continue to happen! And yet being conservative has its place. Because too much liberty, or too fast, causes us to lose Our Balance, and, remember, we have learned that Balance is, indeed, our 6th Sense, and the Key to Our Multi-Sensory Perception of Our Natural 13 Senses, which my fellow nuns and I learned about from the author of *Rain of Gold*. A book, I'd like to add, that I, personally, keep on my bedstand alongside my Bible and the *Diary of Anne Frank*."

And here she stops once again, and once more uses the little hand-embroidered white handkerchief that her grandmother had given her to dry her eyes. And the People, of the People, by the People, for the People, are in awe, in wonderment, feeling so empowered and validated and WHOLE for the FIRST TIME IN THEIR LIVES!

And all around the globe in parks, in back alleys alongside dumpsters, under great trees, and in playgrounds, basketball courts, churches, shopping centers, and in homes, the PEOPLE, of the People, by the People, for the People are listening to Our First Lady Pope's words, and through the Grace of God, her words, spoken in English, are being heard IN EVERY LANGUAGE OF THE WHOLE WORLD!

"Third," she now says, "I'd like to share with you that my fellow Lady Cardinals and Bishops, with whom I've been communicating through computer Skype for weeks, have finally come to the understanding—guided by Jesus and Mary, of course—that this Spiritual Movement of ours, in order to manifest, is not going to be a gradual event.

"IT MUST BE A LIGHTNING BOLT EVENT! A GLOBAL OCCURRENCE OF SUCH MAGNITUDE OF LOVE AND GRATITUDE AND ACCEPTANCE OF EACH OTHER'S BELIEFS AND LIFESTYLES, that it can no more be stopped than us thinking that we can stop A HURRICANE! A FLASH FLOOD! A METEORITE! For we are all equally, equally, equally Children of God! No exceptions! And … and our beloved Anne Frank said it best in her diary—even as they exterminated her people—that she still believed that PEOPLE WERE BASICALLY GOOD OF HEART!"

Once more she uses her little white Irish linen handkerchief.

"This is our mantra," she adds. "Love, Gratitude, and the understanding that we, the PEOPLE, of the People, by the People, for the People are basically ALL GOOD of Heart, and so we have it within us to lead ourselves for the Greater Glory of God! For remember, Our Lord Jesus told us that what He did, we would do more, and that time in our Godelution has come and it's RIGHT NOW! RIGHT HERE! IN OUR FOREVER ETERNAL PRESENT!

"Fourth, and this is a very important and far reaching one," she says, taking in another deep breath. "From this day forth, we will be Totally Transparent, meaning that in financial matters all will be made public and kept public like any reputable nonprofit organization, and along these lines there will also no longer be any tolerance for abusive behavior from any member of Our Church financially, sexually, and/or any other way, for that matter!"

She coughs.

She swallows.

She clears her throat, then suddenly grabs the podium with both hands.

"And what does this mean?" she asks. "It means that Our Beloved Mother Church will no longer be a safe haven for... for arrogant, self-centered spenders or child molesters! It means that there will be no more secrecy, no more moving a molester from one of our Churches to another, and instead, we will... immediately call the authorities and fully cooperate so that the abusing person will be prosecuted to the FULLEST EXTENT OF THE LAW!"

She stops.

She stops, and then continues with tears streaming down her face. "In the past some of my fellow nuns have been intimidated, beaten, and in some cases even... even raped and then murdered to keep them from going to the authorities. And not just by the priests, but also, I'm sad to say, with the participation of some of my fellow nuns. Good nuns. Fine people. And yet out of fear, out of terror of retaliation, cooperated... just like in Germany, in Italy, in Spain when good decent people cooperated with the Nazis.

"You see, it's time for us to stop all our finger-pointing and understand that it isn't... that it isn't just Our Own Beloved Church where such horrors have been committed and are still being committed as we speak, but... but to understand that all male-based, male-controlled institutions and governments have been guilty of some such horrendous abuses worldwide, and it's still going on today where... where young boys and girls—even small children—are being kidnapped, stolen, and sold as sex slaves.

"And why does this happen? Why? Because these are terrible people who do these kidnappings? OH, NO! It's because there is a market for these atrocities! Meaning that there are people of means who make it worthwhile for poor local people to do this kidnapping and stealing. Oh, yes! And … and more times than not, it's done by young men from wealthy, educated parents, who have witnessed the breakdown of their own family, and … and also have seen that greed and corruption are realities of our world that fully approves of war and killing and, of course, rape. So in order to fit in, they purchase, or help in the kidnapping, and then, in more recent years, photograph their abuses and tortures, and killings.

"And now before you start dismissing, accusing, and finger pointing so you can regain your composure, understand … please understand that these individuals come from the same mentality as drunken, abusive parties in colleges and universities, and … and the purchase of exotic foods like monkey brains, and laughing about it. The same people who slaughtered the vast herds of buffalo and bragged and laughed about only eating the tongues. The exotic royal meals, where last century, our fine royalty of Europe relished eating hummingbird breasts and tongues, saying that they'd never tasted anything as delicious!

"So, then, I ask you: who are these people? And I say that they are us; you, me, we, all of us, and then I also ask who are the young boys and girls and children who bring the highest prices, and are also our most vulnerable? Eh, who? Yes, of course, Native People, the Indigenous population from all across my own country of the United States in places like Montana, California, Utah, Texas, across the border from Texas and Arizona, and then in New York, Chicago, Los Angeles, and Italy, Spain, across North Africa and Asia and … and the whole world!

"OH, THE HORRORS that young people have shared with us that happened to them! Places where 6 to 8 girls out of 10 are abused and raped before the age of 12! And many of their friends murdered! And their holocaust isn't even acknowledged, except for a few of our fellow brave nuns and priests, who weren't and still aren't afraid to step forward and make a difference, even if it means going against our Church's archaic position of so often finding it most advantageous to ignore the abuses of the rich and powerful."

She stops.

She can't go on.

She raises her right hand and closes her eyes, once more breathing deeply, again and again.

And there is Silence. Holy, Attentive, United, Sacred Silence across the WHOLE WORLD as the People, of the People, by the People, for the People truly now go within themselves and examine their Hearts and Souls. For they can, now, clearly see that yes, we, Human Begins, might, indeed, be basically good people, and yet just like the Nazis, we, too, are capable of doing and/or allowing horrendous atrocities to happen.

And now with this Monumental Historical Event of the changing of the guard for all of Humanity, people are Awakening to the razor-sharp sword of who we, Human Beings, really are, just as happened on our 6 Sister Planets when they, too, finally had instant global communications, and therefore were able to TRANSFORM!

And this Holy, Attentive, United, Sacred Silence deepens.

In every Church.

In every town center.

In every school.

In every shopping center.

In every home and park and back alley alongside a dumpster around the world—for Our Beloved Mother Earth, herself, is Stirring. Awakening. Feeling Hopeful at long last that her Beloved Children are Awakening. And so with GREAT JOY, OUR MOTHER EARTH SMILES, sending Healing Love*Amor* Energy to her Twin Sister who...who instantly Feels it. Smiles. And also Begins Stirring! Awakening! And...and all across Our Entire Universe—One United Verse, One United Song—this FEELING BETWEEN TWIN SISTER PLANETS REACHES OUT TO THE FURTHEST REACHES OF OUR

FOREVER EXPANDING-CONTRACTING-EXPLODING-
IMPLODING CREATION CREATING!
Our First Lady Pope now opens her eyes and also smiles.
And the Pure Love*Amor* Energy of her Smiles GOES VIRAL
AROUND THE WORLD!
YES! OH, YES!
Our First Lady Pope has, herself, ShapeShifted! SongShifted!
Into BEING the Spirit of the Heart and Soul, Mind and Body of
OUR BELOVED MOTHER EARTH!
And the People—of the People, by the People, for the People
can feel it! Can see it in her SMILE! Her GLOW! Her whole entire
BEING!

"And this," she says as she glances around smiling her great
beautiful smile, "is exactly how we are going to turn around our
whole abusive situation that's nothing new, and has been happening for centuries and centuries, by forgiving and sending love to
ourselves and everyone else. So yes, yes, yes, we can do this. *Si se
puede!* Yes, we can! With all our Hearts and Souls and Faith in God,
I shout, YES! YES! YES! 1,000 MILLION TIMES YES! We can do
it! We can turn things around!

"Look," she continues excitedly, "a few years back I read an
article how the young male elephants had formed groups, because
their fathers and other older male elephants had been slaughtered
for their tusks that were shipped to the wealthy across the whole
world. Not just to China. And so without the guidance of their
fathers and uncles and other older male elephants, these young
groups of male elephants ran rampant, raping young and old
female elephants and even female hippos. It was a phenomenon.
Nothing like this had ever been seen before. Elephants had always
been considered civilized and well-behaved. Photos were taken for
study, and ... and what happened? These photos of rape and abuse
and sometimes actual killings quickly also found a lucrative black
market. The article ended with explaining they now knew just
how fragile elephant nature really is, and how, without the loving,
respectful guidance of strong older males, young male elephants

can lose, in one generation, what had previously been thought of as 'elephant nature'.

"So, yes, I have high hopes for us that fathers, uncles, older brothers and cousins will now step forward, along with grandfathers, in the Spirit of being Sacred Elders as is so well shown again and again in the *Rain of Gold* trilogy, and, of course, used to be true in all Native Cultures. And I have high hopes that these men will come forward, not with admiration for greed and violence, but with the profound understanding of what Leon Shenandoah of the Six Nations Iroquois Confederacy said, 'I, myself, have no power. It's the people behind me who have the power. But if you're asking about strength, not power, then I can say that my greatest strength is gentleness.'

"These words are the words that our youth need to hear and, yes, understand, especially our boys who, with their testosterone, can be so full of energy and want to quickly engage in living, and…and do not have their own blood connection every month with Our Beloved Guiding Mother Moon.

"And we have had many such male leaders of Heart and Soul. Cesar Chavez, who, in the face of insurmountable odds, said, '*Si se puede*'. Yes, we can, and a whole nation rallied to his cause of helping our men and women and even children who toiled in our sun-baked fields, planting and harvesting the very foods we eat. And for me and my Kentucky family, the man who brought it home for us in the most elegant and beautiful way, needs no introduction. His immortal words speak volumes! 'Float like a butterfly! Sting like a bee!' I ask you, how much more can a man be in tune with the Balanced Compassionate Feminine Energy that we are now entering into for the next 26,000 years!

"And so, of course, it will be men like these who will also be Popes in the future, and as I see it, I personally do believe that in our future it will be, more-or-less, a ratio of 5 women to 1 man for our Popes, and also maybe even for our Cardinals and Bishops of Our Church. This is my opinion. This has not yet been run through our staff and made official."

She stops once again, breathes deeply, and closes her eyes.

"Fifth," she says, "I'd now like for all of us to close our eyes. Yes, close our eyes and place both of our hands over our heart and ... and gently go within ourselves and realize that just like the seed of an oak ... has all the Knowledge within it ... that it needs to know how to sprout and grow into a GREAT MAGNIFICENT OAK TREE, so do we, each of us, with the Blessing of God, have within us all the Knowledge ... all the Knowledge that we need to know to grow into MAGNIFICENT HUMAN BEINGS!

"And this is EXACTLY why Pope Francis is endorsing, whole-heartedly, Our Movement of the Vatican from Rome to Ireland for 100 years, then to Mexico for another 100 years, and so forth, so that this can ensure that YES! YES! YES! We, the TRUE FOLLOWERS OF OUR LORD JESUS, can and will, indeed, grow and BLOSSOM INTO MAGNIFICENT HUMAN BEINGS OF THE PEOPLE, BY THE PEOPLE, FOR THE PEOPLE!

"And as such, I ask you, do we the People, of the People, by the People, for the People want to keep the idea that our children are born with original sin? Or, for that matter, with any sin or spiritual imper-fection? These are the type of questions that we will also be addressing.

"And I'd also like to ask us, the People, of the People, by the People, for the People do we want to keep 10 commandments that tell us what not to do, or ... or would we like to replace them with suggestions on what to do in order to live a good, healthy, loving, compassionate life?

"Also, we will no longer cause ourselves any such embarrassing situations as when the Church called Galileo a heretic and impris-oned him, and even though shortly afterwards it was well known that we and our planet were not the center of the universe, it wasn't until recently that we reversed our excommunication. It's obvious why Catholics have been leaving Our Beloved Church in droves. We have been stuck in out-of-date dogma and arrogance and self-serving indoctrination.

"And yet I'd like to also add that these are not questions or matters that we are in a hurry to answer. In fact, we have been thinking, feeling that it might best for us to wait for a whole new generation of children, who have been educated in our schools with Our Full Natural Multi-Sensory Perception, to address these questions. For there, among these children, lays OUR FUTURE LADY POPES! CARDINALS! BISHOPS! PRIESTS! And, of course, NUNS! And now... all of them are free to be celibate, married, or whatever."

She smiles.

She smiles and laughs.

"But, of course," she suddenly shouts, "our immediate GREATEST BIGGEST CHANGE IS THAT we are bringing CHOCOLATE CHIP COOKIES AND WARM MILK TO THE WHOLE WORLD!"

PEOPLE GO WILD!

APPLAUDING!

CHEERING!

WHISTLING!

Then after a few moments, she raises up her hands for silence, and she now says, "Sixth, and certainly not last, I'd now like everyone to turn to the person to the left of you, then to the person on the right of you, and hold hands, looking at each other in the eyes. Then softy, gently, welcome them with all your Heart and Soul into our Shared New, Brave, Kind, Loving, Compassionate, Accepting World. Yes, take your time and do this. We are in no hurry. Good. Good. Excellent. And now gently, softly touch foreheads, and say to each other that 'You are, in fact, another me, and I am, in fact, another you'. For we are ALL! ALL! ALL FAMILY! FAMILY! FAMILY THE WHOLE WORLD OVER!"

She stops.

She stops and waits for everyone to do this. She, too, is in no hurry.

"Okay," she finally says, "everyone now please place your right hand over your heart and raise your left hand, palm open and up to the sky, and say, using your full name, 'I, so and so, now take a solemn oath, within my womb of Creation, to help our Almighty God Create a world where it is easier to be kind, compassionate, all-inclusive, and GOOD OF HEART!'

The People—of the People, by the People, for the People do so, and … and there isn't a dry eye in the whole Luscious Green Valley, inside of the little cute Church, and all up and down the whole valley.

And Enya, Madonna, Lady Gaga, Joan Baez, Carol King, Cher, and everyone begin to sing, 'WE'VE GOT THE WHOLE WORLD IN OUR HANDS! WE'VE GOT THE WHOLE WHOLE WHOLE WORLD IN OUR HANDS!"

And from all around Our Sacred Holy Planet Mother Earth the People—of the People, by the People, for the People join them—in Mexico from on top of the pyramids with Santana BLOWING HIS MAGNIFICENT HORN and in Peru at Machu Picchu and in England at Stonehenge and in Africa at the Great Pyramids and in China at the Great Wall and EVERYWHERE AROUND OUR BELOVED HOLY MOTHER EARTH ALL ALL ALL HER CHILDREN ARE AWAKENEING AND REACHING FOR OUR SACRED FATHER SKY

AND IT'S BEAUTIFUL!

BEAUTIFUL!

BEAUTIFUL!

WE HAVE ARRIVED!

WE HAVE FINALLY ARRIVED!

And now OUR STAR COUSINS, who have ShapeShifted, SingShifted into Human Earth Form, add, "WE'VE GOT THE WHOLE UNIVERSE IN OUR HANDS! WE'VE GOT THE WHOLE-WIDE-UNIVERSE IN OUR HANDS!"

AND SO IT IS!

ACHILDREN!

AWOMEN!

AMEN!

ASTAR COUSINS!

MI CASA ES SU CASA

O ne of my warmest and fondest memories growing up on our *ranchito* is how my parents would always greet people at our front door, saying "Mi casa es su casa" which translates in English to "my house is your house." And they'd really mean it, letting our guests immediately know that they could feel comfortable to act as if they were in their own home and not just visiting guests.

In other words, in the context of the book you have just read, "mi casa es su casa" is my way of reminding each of us that my Vision is your Vision, and my Home is your Home, and whether you are Catholic, Protestant, Jewish, Muslim, Sikh or a non believer altogether, the time has come in Our Collective Godelution for us to drop our weapons and words of separation, place our two hands behind our backs and bend forward gently touching foreheads, then look into each others eyes, and say "You are another me, and I am another you, and we are both equally children of God." This is our future! This is what our 6 Sister Planets did, and remember, they were even more lost and violent than us.

You see, we are living in a perilous time. There has never been so much fear, so much disharmony, so much everyone out just for themselves. And yet we are also living in a miraculous time. In other words, there has never been a better time for all of us to come together and honor our planet Mother Earth with all our Hearts and Souls!

A few months ago all over the world we experienced a profound eclipse of the sun by the moon. This was a unique astronomical event, one that comes only once every fifty to one hundred years with the clarity that occurred, and also we have recently been experiencing tremendous earthquakes, tornadoes, and flash floods all over the globe. Simply, Our Mother Earth is alive and she's telling us she's sick and suffering.

Also my Native American Grandmothers explained to me that our Mother Moon is the Contracting Healing Compassionate Feminine Energy of the Universe, and our Father Sun is the Aggressive Expanding Exploding Male Energy of the Universe. Without the Sun we cannot live, and without the Moon we also cannot live. Too much Sun, too much masculine energy, leads to destruction. Too much Moon, too much feminine energy, leads to an imbalance.

So what we need to once more do is to bring back Balance between Our Masculine and Feminine Energies so that Our Mother Moon and Father Sun and Our Beloved Mother Earth can once again be in Tune, in Harmony with the Grand Glorious SYMPHONY OF OUR FOREVER CONTRACTING EXPANDING UNIVERSE!

This is what my two Indigenous Mamagrandes told me, then further explained to me that Our First Lady Pope will help unite the Nurturing Feminine Heart and Soul Healing Love*Amor* Energy that our modern world so desperately needs at this time.

Since our trip to Spain in 1992, every year on the Sunday before Thanksgiving, we have an event called Snow Goose Global Thanksgiving at our Rancho Villaseñor in Oceanside, California that starts at 1pm and goes to sunset, when we light candles and face east sending Our United Love*Amor* Healing Energy around Our Beloved Mother Earth. Well over 1,000 people attend every year coming from all over the United States, Canada, and Mexico, and we've had groups come in from Australia, India, China, and Africa. It's a day of giving thanks. No talk about politics, religion, or sports. Bus loads come. Some people have been coming every year for over fifteen years. People get high on giving thanks. People get high on seeing each other as Children of God. Problems disappear. Borders dissolve. It's a potluck. Bring a dish made with Love*Amor* with your own two hands for twelve. There will be music and laughter and people painting kids faces and whirling around like Snow Geese Angels of ourselves! TRULY, MI CASA ES SU CASA!

CAN YOU FEEL IT?

CAN YOU FEEL IT?

THERE'S NOTHING WE CAN DO TO STOP WORLD HARMONY AND PEACE AND ABUNDANCE FOR ALL!

YES! YOU DO FEEL IT! IT'S PART OF OUR DNA!

LOOK! YOU GOT A SMILE ON YOUR FACE AND A TWINKLE IN YOUR EYES!

Thank you, gracias!

Victor E. Villaseñor

P.S. Also contact us about starting your very own Snow Goose Global Thanksgiving. Remember, according to the Mayan Calendar and many other Indigenous Calendars around the world, we have a Window of Timeless Time between December 21st, 2012 and November 10th, 2026, 3pm California time for us to plant Our Feminine Seeds of Love*Amor* for the next 26,000 years, and this includes the manifestation of Our First Lady Pope and moving the Vatican from Rome to Ireland ACCOMPANIED BY OUR INTERPLANETARY MUSICAL OF CREATION CREATING!

BONUS PAGES

MEET THE AUTHOR

Victor Edmundo Villaseñor was born in 1940 in the old barrio of Carlsbad, California about one mile from the ocean and half a mile south of present-day old town Carlsbad. For the first four years of his life he was raised primarily by his Yaqui Indian grandmother, Doña Guadalupe, a native Mexican.

The summer before starting kindergarten, Victor and his family moved three miles north to South Oceanside where he still resides today. He started school at the old grammar school behind the Oceanside High School, and in the third grade he was transferred to the new grammar school on Cassidy Street in South Oceanside. After that he attended two different Catholic schools, and a military academy in Carlsbad.

School was extremely difficult for Victor, not only because of severe dyslexia, but also because of the worldview that he'd acquired from his grandmother, parents, and the Mexican Indian workers on the ranch, with whom he often felt more at home than he did with the people outside the ranch gates.

By a stroke of luck he was able to attend the newly opened Catholic University of San Diego, where he met several gifted professors and priests. For the first time Victor was able to discuss the things that had been haunting him all his life; it was a turning point. He then traveled to Mexico, found his roots, and returned to the United States a changed person. In the wild open spaces of Wyoming, he had a vision and decided to devote his life to writing. He wrote for a couple of years, went into the army, came out, and continued writing. A few years later he ran across an ad for a creative writing course offered by the University of California Extension. But the ad was only for advanced writers who had been published or who had been working as professional writers for at least a year.

Victor was terror-stricken, but realizing that he needed help, he packed ten boxes of unpublished manuscripts and short stories into the back of his truck. He hoped that the bulk of his work might impress the professor enough to allow him into the course.

When it was Victor's turn to tell the professor what credentials he had that would make him worthy of being accepted into the writing course, tears came to his eyes. He simply said, "I've been writing for six years and I have about five hundred pounds of my writing in my truck to show you."

Most of the people in the classroom were professional newspaper and magazine writers, and a few had had a book or two published—many started laughing, but the professor didn't. "Where's your truck?" he asked in a serious tone of voice. At break time he walked with Victor out to his vehicle to take a look. There in that parking lot, he began a lifelong relationship with Mr. Ronald Kayser from La Jolla, a professional pulp- fiction writer who'd had more than two hundred books published in his time.

A few years later when Victor still could not get published, Mr. Kayser showed him an ad for the Creative Writing Department at UCLA, headed by Dr. Savage. Victor knew he didn't have the credentials to get into UCLA, so he sat in Dr. Savage's office for three days in his attempt to get into the classes. Finally the head of the department agreed to see him.

"You see, sir," he told the well dressed elegant man, "I was told that you have the best creative writing department in the nation and I don't have the credentials to get into your school, but you see, I need to become a great writer because my people don't have a voice. In fact, my family's stories are ridiculed, or at best called Indian superstition. And all the successful cultures of our planet have a written voice. The Jews have their Bible, and no matter how wild their stories are, they aren't ridiculed. And the Greeks have *The*

Odyssey, the Irish have their writers, and so do the Germans, the French, the English, and the Chinese and Japanese. Do you see, everyone needs a voice that gives heart and soul to their people, sir." Tears were streaming down his face. "And nine years ago I took an oath before God to give my people, the Natives of America, a voice, and I've written and finished more than eight books, sixty five short stories, and ten plays, but I'm still not good enough yet, and so I need to get into your department, sir."

"What's your name?" asked Dr. Savage.

"Victor Villaseñor," he said.

"How do you spell it?" he asked.

Victor spelled his name and Dr. Savage gave him a handwritten note saying that Victor was a personal friend of his and his family, and that if any professors had any room in their class to please let him sit in. This is when Victor made another lifelong friendship with Dr. Mueller, the playwriting professor at UCLA. Between Mueller and Kayser, Victor was finally ushered into the world of professional writing after more than 265 rejections. His works were immediately compared to the best of John Steinbeck and Gabriel Garcia Marquez, two of the greatest writers of the 20th Century.

WHY WRITE?

I write because if I didn't, I'd go crazy*loco*. Writing is my healing experience. It gives me the opportunity to re-digest my life, like a cow chewing her cud—a peace comes over me and I realize that maybe I'm not such a dumb, inadequate guy after all, and my family isn't so bad either. This inner peace lightens me up and gives me the strength and confidence to go on in life, and sometimes I'm even able to see that my bumbling mistakes are funny and not that bad. In fact, by the tenth or twelfth rewrite of the same material, I start to see—guess what—we're all heroes! Every one of us! We just need the time to chew over our stuff and gain a new perspective.

My mother was shocked when I told her that I wanted to write a book about my father and her. She told me that she was a nobody, that her life wasn't important, but then as she read my tenth or fifteenth draft she said to me that she could now begin to see that everyone's life is important and that her own mother and father had been great people.

This is why I write, to bring this new perspective to our lives, returning us all to a yesteryear when all over the world we felt that we were living in the Grace of Creation itself! Try it. Write about yourself and your loved ones with all your Heart and Soul, being truthful, and yet generous, and you, too, will then see that your loved ones are good people.

And the name of the game isn't just about getting published. The name of the game is about healing yourself and believing that you are, indeed, wonderful beyond your wildest dreams. Believe me, without chewing over our daily events like the cow chewing her cud in a green meadow, life can get us down to the point where we can't even see up from down. Read. Write. Study. Create a journal. It's fun! And discover that you are, indeed, WONDERFUL! MEANING FULL OF WONDER!

IN MY GARAGE

In my garage I have approximately half a ton of manuscripts that have never been published—including *Witness a Man, The Sun Will Die, Jude, Hunger, Cadillac Joe, Hunting Alone, Big Ben, The Poet and the Bull, Stud Stall,* and *Lady and Lucky.* The titles go on and on; some are full-length books and others are short stories. Each of the works might have as many as 10 to 20 different versions. What I was doing, when I wrote all of this, was polishing my craft and trying to find my voice.

Once I went for nearly six months without speaking, trying to get that nasty, negative little voice out of my head and break through into that rich, confident voice I could hear when I read Homer, Cervantes, Melville, Anne Frank, Salinger, Faulkner, Steinbeck,

Hemingway, Azuela, Kazantzakis, and the Russians: Dostoevsky and Tolstoy, who eventually became my greatest influences. These Russians had a passion and a power for raw truth that was different from the other authors I'd been studying. The Russians reminded me of the wild stories that my father told us of his homeland in *Los Altos de Jalisco,* where *tequila* was made and where the *mariachis* were created.

I soon discovered that if I got up at two or three in the morning, the whole world was quiet and I could go outside and speak with the stars, breathing in their power. Then I'd go into my writing room, build a fire in the old cast iron stove and watch the little flames. Soon those tiny dancing flames would draw me into a hypnotic state and I'd be able to get out of my own head, shed my socially-correct skin like a snake, and start writing with all my Heart and Soul. The words would now just pour out of me as if I was connected to the Heavens.

Today, even after fifty years of writing, I still write longhand on blank paper with a No. 2 pencil on a clipboard. For years I preferred yellow paper for my first draft or two because many times I'd write outside in the garden or at the beach, but the sun's glare on white paper got to be too much. I would write if I didn't get paid. I would write if I knew I was going to die tomorrow. In fact, my writing really didn't get good until I gave up all hope of ever getting published and knowing that I could die in peace because I'd done the best I could to give Life to God, meaning the best within me.

The way I see it, it's not enough for us to just live our lives. We need to lift up our Hearts and Souls on a daily basis with the gut-true understanding that it is no accident we are here on this planet at this time. Why? Because we are all Co-Creators with the Almighty once we make ourselves consciously available to the act of Creation.

I never tell a person "Have a nice day." That sounds so lame. I tell people, "Have a great, fantastic day and a juicy, exciting night!" You should see how their eyes light up and their whole energy changes. Truly, it's our job to open up and co-create our lives with excitement and purpose for the greater glory of all living life. And I don't care if you're an atheist or an agnostic or whatever! Just do it! It feels good, deep down inside! Who cares what you think! It's what you do that counts! So kick ass! And start by kicking YOUR OWN ASS FIRST!

DOUBT AND FEAR

Look, fear and doubt can come to us at anytime and in the strangest forms. Take what happened to me in Portland, Oregon about 20 years ago. There I was with two best sellers under my belt and raving reviews from across the whole country, so you'd think that I'd have enough confidence to not become a Doubting Thomas.

But oh, no! There I was in a small luxurious elevator with two people when fear and doubt suddenly came bursting into me with such force that I almost crapped in my pants, and by the time I reached my room, I was ready to puke.

You see, what happened is that I'd given a talk that I'd thought was good at a Portland University that evening. The auditorium had been filled with 1,000s of people and I'd received a standing ovation, and so I'd figured all was great.

But then, after my talk, my sister's childhood friend and her husband took me to their home on the outskirts of Portland. It was a stately old three story mansion. Elegant, and yet kind of dark and spooky looking. We had drinks in a large room before a huge wood burning rock-made fireplace. And this is when my sister's friend calmly turned to me and told me that she'd seen how much the people had really loved my talk. That I'd inspired them, and it was wonderful to see how they'd purchased my book and walked out of the place feeling full of hope and peace for the world.

"But, of course, my husband and I don't buy any of that," she'd added with a grand smile. "Sure, that's a good talk for the public, and I can see that you're being very successful with it, but it has nothing to do with reality."

I was taken back. I didn't know what to think or much less say.

"Look," she continued, "everybody knows that there will always be wars. That even the ancient Civilizations had wars. The Akkadians, Babylonians, Assyrians, Chaldeans. The Jews had wars too. All civilizations have had wars. It's part of our human nature and so we will always keep having them. But you did do a very good marketing job for yourself just as we do with our manufacturing. Toast," she added, holding up her cognac goblet with a big smile.

I toasted with her and her husband, but I was trembling. I felt that I had just been kicked in the gut. And here, I'd thought she and her husband had really understood my talk, especially since she knew *mi familia*.

It was almost midnight when they walked me down the hallway to an elevator. I'd never seen an elevator in a private home before. It was small and had beautifully carved wood. They got in with me and we went up to the third floor. And I don't know how to explain this, but there we were, so close together, surrounded by such luxury and she and her husband looked so well-dressed and successful and...and the cables of the elevator were making such old screeching sounds that I was suddenly filled with terror. Not just fear. But Absolute terror!

I mean, maybe they were right and I was wrong. Sure, of course. They were rich. They were successful. They had, my God, their own private elevator. And what did I have, some old wiggling stairs that were in desperate need of repair. By the time they walked me to my room, I was feeling sick inside. It was a large room with great antique-looking furniture, and king size bed with a beautiful headboard of carved dark wood. Beyond the bed were large gorgeous windows looking out on treetops. It was a full moon and the Heavens were full of small bright white clouds and large patches of dark sky with blinking Stars. Tears came to my eyes. It had taken me 16 years to write *Rain of Gold*. And authors who made money put out a book or two per year. And I wasn't young anymore, and I was still a struggling writer. By the time I got in bed, I was shivering with cold fear. Of course, they were right. No doubt about it. I was a damn fool, and so MY TALKS WERE FULL OF CRAP!

But then in the early morning hours, I awoke and I could feel that my dad and two Ingenious Grandmothers were over by the window, and the moonlight was coming behind them. I sat up and I began to feel that they were transmitting flashes of understanding to me. Yes, of course, those people were right. We had nothing on this planet to give us any indication that we could possibly ever have world peace. So for me to have said last evening that there was nothing we could do to stop us from having World Harmony and Peace and Abundance for All, had, in fact, sounded preposterous. Why? Because, simply, we haven't yet had that experience on our Mother Earth.

I breathed.

I breathed and stayed calm and it was then immediately transmitted into me that we belonged to Six Sister Planets. Yes, Six, and that all of our Six Sister Planets, who had been even more lost and violent than us, had already found World Harmony and Peace and Abundance for All eons and eons of Timeless Time ago.

I smiled.

I laughed.

And I was told to rest, sleep well, and realize that we were right on schedule.

Well, looking back what can I say? Tell you that going up in that little elevator to the third story, I got so full of doubt and fear that I almost shit in my pants. And yet in the morning, when I used that same elevator going down to the ground floor, I felt a peace and confidence and understanding that I'd never felt before in all of my life. Well, that's what happened. Oh, it feels so good to be gifted a much, much larger picture of WHO WE HUMAN BEINGS REALLY ARE!

A HAPPY LITTLE GAME I PLAY

For over 25 years, I have this little game I play every time I leave my home. What I do is say something or do something to make at least 10 people smile and feel better about themselves and the world.

Take for instance what happened yesterday when I was walking across the parking lot at Costco. There, up ahead of me was an elderly lady taking the groceries out of her cart.

"Hello!" I said. "Can I help you?"

"No, thanks," she said. "I can do it."

"Hey, that's a pretty heavy case of bottled water," I added. "At least let me help you with that. Really, I'm not coming on to you. I just want to help."

Well, she was in her late 80s I'm sure and she now stopped what she was doing and turned and looked at me, then with a smile said, "Are you sure that you're not coming on to me?"

And she burst out laughing and laughing. And I started laughing too. So I helped her with her case of water, then helped her arrange all the rest of her things in her car, and we were still laughing and laughing.

"Can I take your cart for you?" I asked.

"Sure, take it."

Then she winked at me as she got in her car, and I winked back.

"I knew it!" she said. "I just knew it! You were coming on to me!"

"Of course," I said. "You're a very beautiful exciting looking girl!"

Well, what can I say? The exchange of Happy, BIG BIG HAPPY ENERGY that happened with that little old lady was FANTASTIC! FABULOUS! AND THE JOY I received with her coquettish wink sent me SHOOTING THROUGH THE HEAVENS! Oh, I hadn't laughed so hard in days! Truly, I know it's a cliché, BUT ONLY IN GIVING WITH ALL OUR HEART AND SOUL DO WE RECEIVE!

Today at our local market I walked up to a mother with two little boys and I said to them, "Hey, guys! You two are Angels! You really really are, and you're wonderful! And I also want you two to know that your parents both came into this world as Angels, too, but then they stressed out, and so they have forgotten. So you two kids need to remind your parents every single day that they are Angels, too!"

"Thank the kind man," the mother said, smiling.

The boys were embarrassed, but still they thanked me.

"Okay, and now tell your mama that she, too, is an Angel! Go on, tell her!"

"YES, TELL ME! TELL ME!" the mom now said excitedly.

The boys did, and oh, their mother's face filled with such Love*Amor* and joy and warmth and appreciation, and the two boys got all goo-goo eyed, too!

Seeing this, I said, "WOW! Just imagine what a different world we'd have if every day we told each other we are Angels! Why, we'd instantly have a kinder, friendlier world! So tonight at the dinner table be sure to tell your dad he's an Angel. In fact, as soon as you get home draw a picture of your dad and mom being Angels! Okay, boys?"

They both said, "OKAY!" with a lot of energy, and I turned to go and the eyes of the two boys kept following me. They'd been HeartTouched!

That same afternoon, I saw a dad pushing a cart at Home Depot and he had two beautiful little girls; one in the cart and another walking alongside him.

"Hey, girls!" I said. "I want you to know that you're both Angels! You really really are! And you're wonderful!"

To my surprise the father snapped at me. "Yeah, sometimes, sure! But not right now!"

I took in a deep breath, closed my eyes, then said, "Excuse me, but all children are always Angels. And so are adults. It's just that we forget. Just look at your two beautiful daughters, and in their eyes you can see how much they love you. So tonight at dinner remind each other that you are, indeed, Angels and that you're all wonderful and you'll feel much better."

The man looked at me. Really looked at me, then took a great big deep breath and blew it out.

"Thank you," he said. "You're right. Thank you very much. It's just been a tough week, now I get home and our toilet is out," he added with laughter.

Like always, I parked my car at the far end of the Smart & Final parking lot so I could get in a good walk, and as I approached the store, I saw this heavy set older man with wild hair get out of a beat up old greyish dirty car from the passenger side. He was grinning and laughing. Then from the driver's side, a heavy set older woman got out, and she, too, had wild looking hair and was grinning and laughing. I smiled. I couldn't help it. They were old and fat and so happy! BIG BIG HAPPY!

Then I noticed that she had a great big yellow purse with a lot of bright colorful flowers painted on it. She shouldered the big purse, and there they were, going towards the store and still laughing and having so much fun together. I followed them into Smart & Final, and they just couldn't stop laughing. At this point, I walked up to them.

"HEY, YOU TWO!" I shouted, "DID YOU KNOW THAT LAUGHTER IS CONTAGIOUS? So you two, by being so happy, are helping make this planet a more wonderful place for EVERYONE! CONGRATULATIONS TO THE TWO OF YOU!"

They laughed even more, saying, "Thank you! Thank you!"

"Where did you get that beautiful purse," I asked the woman.

"We just got back from Hawaii! It's our first real vacation we've ever had in all of our lives! We were saving up for a newer used car until we both said, 'What the hell do we want a newer car for? Let's blow this money!' So we went to Hawaii and now we're stuck with our beat up old car, but, I'll tell you, we had the time of our lives in Hawaii! Didn't we? Eh, honey?" she said, gripping him by the ass, and looking at him in the eyes with such love. "And now we call that old hunk of junk 'Our Beach Throne!' We learned in Hawaii what old cars are really made for."

"Yeah," he said, hugging her close, "we ripped out the backseat and put in a mattress that goes out through the trunk so at sunset we can park at the beach and lay down together as we look out at the sea," he added.

"WOW! THAT'S ONE GREAT STORY! Can I hug you two?"

"Sure," they both said.

And I hugged her and gave her a kiss on the cheek, and the husband then let me hug and kiss him on the cheek, too. And when I got home, I was still laughing and so I TOLD THE STORY TO MY WHOLE FAMILY, AND THEN WE WERE ALL LAUGHING AND LAUGHING!

Last week, I was down at the beach in South Oceanside at the end of Cassidy Street, and there were two little kids playing in the surf. I walked up to them and said, "You're both Angels! AND YOU'RE WONDERFUL!"

A beautiful young woman came running up behind me.

"WE KNOW YOU!" she shouted. "You write children's books! We love them, especially the one about the fart! And you told my kids this same thing last week at Trader Joe's, that they're Angels!" And she hugged me and kissed me. "Since that day, we tell each other at the dinner table every evening that we're Angels and my husband loves it!" she added, giving me another hug and kiss.

So there you have it, this is the little happy game I've been playing for over 25 years every time I leave my home, to say something or do something that will bring a smile and make people feel a little better about themselves and the world. Try it! You'll like it! And if anyone rejects your random-act-of-good-feeling-kindness just thank them and send them Love*Amor* anyway.

You see, this truly is a WIN-WIN SITUATION!

And the big payoff is that after I've spent just a small part of my day in Giving with all my Heart and Soul, then that night I RECEIVE IN ABUNDANCE! I sleep well. I have fantastic wonderful DreamVoyages of great adventures and wake up laughing and BIG BIG HAPPY! TRY IT! YOU'LL LOVE IT! IN FACT, IT'S CONTAGIOUS! LOOK, I'M 78 AND MOST OF THE TIME I FEEL AS EXCITED AND ENERGETIC AS A TEENAGER!

APPLE PIE AND CHOCOLATE CHIP COOKIES

By the way, this year at our Snow Goose Global Thanksgiving Celebration, we're going to have an apple pie and chocolate chip cookie baking contest. You see, my mother Lupe made the greatest apple pies I've ever tasted, and I MISS THEM SO MUCH! They were tart. Not too sweet. And the apples weren't overcooked. And the crust, underneath and on the top, wasn't thick, and yet very tasty. I think it was layered. I don't really know. And then she'd add to the apples cinnamon and a little bit of brown sugar or honey, and there were little roundish black things with tiny little tails, possibly cloves. But people tell me that this can't be so. Who knows? All I know is that her pies were so delicious and I haven't had a good piece of apple pie since my mother passed over in the year 2000. So bring your apple pies and the best pies will each get a free house tour and a brand new autographed copy of *Our First Lady Pope* book, and please note that members of our local Fire Department will be the apple pie tasters, along with some children.

Also remember, Our First Lady Pope's first promise when the Vatican moves from Rome to Ireland is to bake the best chocolate chip cookies in all the world, BECAUSE IT'S GOING TO TAKE

A LOT OF CHOCOLATE CHIP COOKIES AND WARM MILK TO CREATE SMILES AND GIVE US A KINDER FRIENDLIER WORLD!

So yes, of course, in order to help her we need to also have a chocolate chip cookie baking contest this year at our Snow Goose Global Thanksgiving. And we need to send boxes of cookies along with a book of *Our First Lady Pope* to all the people at the Vatican, and to the Mother of God Church in Kentucky, and yes, to your own local priests and nuns and ministers in all our different religious denominations around the world, and to Enya, of course, and to Madonna and Lady Gaga and Oprah and J.K. Rowling and Whoopi Goldberg and Jason Mraz—the only celebrity that I have met and who instantly understood this Global Vision—and my personal mentors, Sonny Rollins and Santana.

You see, what we need to do is to prepare the world for Our First Lady Pope and this is where you, me, we, all of us can help by sending eBooks and real books along with a box of the best chocolate chip cookies in all the world to our local TV Stations, Radio Stations, to everyone you can think of and, of course, also share through Social Media around the globe, so we can start out our New Year well on our way CREATING A KINDER, FRIENDLIER WORLD!

JUMP ABOARD! We're all together on THE SAME SPACESHIP CALLED MOTHER EARTH! And Our First Lady Pope is Singing! Dancing! Shouting! "SHARE ME! STEAL ME! BUY ME! DO WHATEVER IT TAKES TO JUST GIVE YOU, ME, WE, ALL OF US A CHANCE—AND WE'RE HOME FREE!"

MI CASA ES SU CASA! AND WE ARE ALL, ALL, ALL *FAMILIA*!

Made in the USA
San Bernardino, CA
09 December 2017